The DNA of
Physician-Leadership

The DNA of Physician-Leadership

Creating Dynamic Executives

Myron J. Beard, PhD
Steve Quach, MD

BUSINESS EXPERT PRESS

The DNA of Physician-Leadership: Creating Dynamic Executives
Copyright © Business Expert Press, LLC, 2020.

First published in 2020 by
Business Expert Press, LLC
222 East 46th Street, New York, NY 10017
www.businessexpertpress.com

ISBN-13: 978-1-94999-190-1 (paperback)
ISBN-13: 978-1-94999-191-8 (e-book)

Business Expert Press Health Care Management Collection

Collection ISSN: 2333-8601 (print)
Collection ISSN: 2333-861x (electronic)

Cover image licensed by Ingram Image, StockPhotoSecrets.com
Cover and interior design by S4Carlisle Publishing Services Private Ltd., Chennai, India

First edition: 2020

10 9 8 7 6 5 4 3 2 1

Printed in the United States of America.

Abstract

Increasingly, physicians are transitioning away from being clinicians to becoming health care leaders and administrators. While the reasons for this transition are varied (e.g., attractive opportunities, lifestyle choices, personal growth, burnout), the journey to leadership positions is fraught with new and unexpected challenges. It comes *without a roadmap*. Virtually no training is provided in medical school for the consideration that these physicians may move into leadership positions. In fact, many of the skills they have developed in medical school have narrowed their focus and created very specialized experts. Such specialized skills can actually interfere with preparation for broader leadership positions. Physicians with MBAs are becoming increasingly common, and yet they still find themselves underprepared for the challenges of physician-leadership. *The DNA of Physician-Leadership* serves to fill that important gap. *The DNA of Physician-Leadership* is a practical, step-by-step guide for health care professionals, providing them the necessary tools required to be successful in leadership positions, including:

- Understanding typical physician psychology
- Comprehending health care as a business
- Learning the essence of leadership
- Creating high-performing teams
- Delegating for impact
- Setting a compelling vision
- Communicating with influence
- Negotiating successfully

This book comes from real-life examples and experiences. It is complete with case studies, exercises, and a unique **Coach's Corner**, summarizing each chapter and providing specific suggestions for leadership development. In addition, we provide significant insights into the typical personalities of physicians and what they will need to change or modify to become successful leaders. We believe that no such practical guide currently exists in the literature. The audience for our book includes physicians who are already in leadership positions or considering transitioning into them.

Keywords

leadership; health care; medical leadership; hospital; health; administrators; organization; management; health care management; health care leadership; health care administration; physician-leader; physician-leadership; physician executive; communication; conflict; negotiation; delegation; goal setting; vision; team; team building

Contents

Acknowledgments

The writing of this book would not have been possible without the help of several important people to whom I am very grateful. First and foremost, my thanks go to Scott Isenberg, managing executive editor of Business Expert Press, for having the confidence in us to support the writing and publication of this book. Without his support and encouragement, we would not have been able to proceed. Likewise, I give most hearty thanks to my coauthor, Steve Quach. It was initially Steve's idea that a book for physician-leaders would be a valuable contribution to the field of physician-leadership. It was a pleasure to work side by side with Steve as we collaborated on just what the book would include. I am especially thankful to my amazing wife, Ann, who offered her critical eye and seasoned editing skills in the editing of each chapter. In addition, we thank our dear friend and colleague, Helen Resnik, who initially introduced us to each other. Without this introduction, the book would never have been conceived. Many thanks also go to my much-appreciated sons, Andrew and Matthew, for their willingness to read select material and provide their wise input. Last but not least, I thank Alan Weiss, my coauthor of a previous book, *The DNA of Leadership*. Alan's initial introduction to Business Expert Press made possible that book, and this one. In addition, Alan has been a great mentor and teacher, from whom I have learned a great deal about the world of consulting and leadership.

—Myron Beard

It is my honor to have coauthored this book on a subject that is so near and dear to my heart. Firstly, I am indebted to my coauthor, Myron Beard. His incredible knowledge of leadership and experience as an author was what made this book possible. I am thankful for all of the leaders who have been my role models and shaped me as a leader. Among them, Donna Sollenberger, Dr. Thomas Blackwell, and Dr. Carl Getto deserve special mention for providing me with the solid foundations of leadership. I would also like to thank Dr. Lindsay Sonstein and Dr. Brian Dwinnell for reviewing the manuscript and providing valuable input. Special appreciation goes to Shawn Donahue, who provided assistance with all of the graphics and artwork.

My deepest gratitude goes to my family, who truly made this book possible. I am thankful to my parents, Hoa and Loann Quach, who always supported me despite the many sacrifices they made along the way. My wife, Dr. Pamela Havlen, is a saint for being my sounding board both in life and for this book, all while leading our family and her own successful career. Ethan and Charlotte, my dear children, are the inspiration for me to be a better person, father, and leader.

—Steve Quach

Introduction and Overview

Physicians have always been the inherent leaders of the clinical health care team. Many physicians are drawn to leadership beyond that of the clinical team. These aspiring physician-leaders are called to duty for a variety of reasons. Some have a passion to lead people and organizations. Some hope to create a positive impact on health care beyond the patients they personally care for. Others are desirous of change and look to leadership as an alternative to clinical medicine.

Undoubtedly, change is a constant in health care. This has always been true and is perhaps more true today than ever before. Physicians are not immune to this change. On the contrary, they are at its epicenter. Despite their central role in health care, most physicians feel as if they are enduring change as opposed to driving it. They struggle with electronic medical records that do not meet their needs or those of their patients. At times, it can feel like administrators and insurance companies rule their lives with endless regulations, limitations, and preauthorizations.

It is the increasing complexity of health care delivery systems that has led to this state of affairs. Within this new reality of health care lies both an opportunity for physicians and an urgency for the system itself. More physicians must transcend their traditional clinical roles in favor of leadership positions. Physician-leaders have long possessed enormous potential and carry with them great hope for all of health care. Although this potential has yet to fully materialize, the ranks of physician-leaders continue to swell, and the need is greater than ever.

As physicians answer the call of leadership, they encounter unanticipated challenges that will test both their aptitude and their fortitude. This should be no surprise. There is no formal training or path to physician-leadership. The very training, experience, and perspective that make physicians uniquely qualified to lead also constrain their development and ultimate success as physician-leaders. As a result, most new physician-leaders struggle with effectiveness, happiness, or both. We know this from personal experience. This was our inspiration for writing this book.

We scoured our decades of combined leadership experience in health care to select the topics that most specifically apply to physician-leaders and narrowed those down to the absolute essentials. Our goal is not only to arm physician-leaders with the tools that success demands but also to make the transition for physician-leaders a little less foreign and a lot less painful.

Nearly every chapter contains a case study that provides a real-life illustration of the concepts contained within that chapter. Each chapter concludes with a "Coach's Corner," which is a set of practical exercises intended to assist you in applying the concepts of the chapter to your own development. The final chapter contains answers to the questions most frequently asked by aspiring physician-leaders as well as a set of leadership pearls that we have harvested over the course of our careers.

The underlying theme of this book is balance, versatility, and individualization. No one leader is exactly like the next. Only through deep introspection and true acceptance of your unique strengths and opportunities can you apply the lessons within these pages to their full effect.

We hope that you find our observations to be both helpful and comforting in your leadership journey.

SECTION 1

Foundations
of Physician-Leadership

CHAPTER 1

Migrating to Physician-Leadership: An Introduction

In a recent *Forbes* article, the authors observed that shaping the future of health care depends on physician-leaders (Price and Norbeck 2017). They stated that physicians stand at the intersection of the often-competing cultures of patient care and business. They added that physicians are increasingly moving into titled leadership positions. However, it is often the case that physicians are ill-prepared to move into these high-level positions. In fact, the very skills that are required for a physician to be a great clinician often compete with or undermine the skills required to be a great leader. Further, the historical tension between clinicians and administrators compounds the challenge of physicians moving into leadership roles. In fact, transitioning into health care leadership is sometimes referred to as "going to the dark side." That said, physicians *can* successfully transition into health care roles. The physician-leaders who successfully make this transition are among the most effective leaders in health care. We have found that there are certain critical skills that physicians must learn to become most effective as they consider transitioning into leadership roles. This is the foundation for this book.

The Business of Health Care: From Bedside to Boardroom

Physicians spend years in medical school and residency learning how to take care of patients. Through this education and continuing into practice, physicians are taught essential medical knowledge and trained how to think clinically. They are the leaders of the clinical health care team, but most physicians were never taught basic administrative and leadership skills. They understand almost every facet of the health care system from the clinical perspective, yet most do not understand the fundamental business models of health care.

During their careers, many physicians will have the opportunity to be medical directors or department chairs. These leadership roles are usually part-time and often rotate from one physician to another. Balancing these administrative positions with a busy clinical load creates significant stress. This often leads physicians to leave these leadership roles in favor of pure clinical practice. Some bounce back and forth between the clinical role and the hybrid clinical/administrative role multiple times, especially early in their careers. Those physicians who have both a passion for leadership and are able to acquire the necessary nonclinical leadership skills often progress to full-time administrative roles such as chief medical officer (CMO) or chief executive officer (CEO). At this stage, physicians usually do not migrate back to clinical practice because it is very difficult to maintain or regain clinical competency (Figure 1.1).

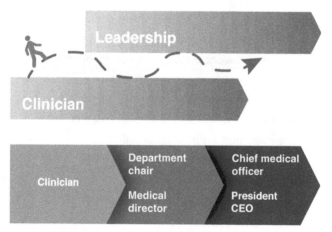

Figure 1.1 The parallel paths of the physician-leader

Although the paths of the clinical physician and the physician-leader are parallel, the roles in each path require vastly different skills. The skills necessary in a clinical setting do not require the same level of relationship management, strategic thinking, or business acumen as do leadership roles. We provide the tools and insights required to make this transition successfully, broadening the skill sets learned in either medical training or clinical practice.

Leadership Transition: From Star Player to Team Captain

Although the patient is always the ultimate decision maker in their own care, the physician is at the center of the health care team's decision making and execution. Despite recent work in the area of crew resource management and shared decision making, most physicians still practice as the authoritative leaders of the clinical team. This is not surprising because physicians are taught that the ultimate responsibility for the patient rests on their shoulders. This is reinforced by the clinical health care system, which looks to the physician as the final authority as well as the medical liability environment, which is highly focused on the physician. In the clinical setting, the physician is the quarterback of the health care team. The quarterback, although surrounded and supported by the rest of the team, is the one who calls the plays in the huddle and often has to make the play work once the ball is snapped. The quarterback is often the hero when the game is won and the goat when the game is lost.

In contrast, when physicians move to broader leadership roles, like medical director or department chair, the very behaviors that made them successful in the clinical role can be their undoing. The role of the physician-leader is less that of a doer or commander. It is more about influencing and leveraging others. Physician-leaders need to learn how to inspire, develop others, and align those under their management around a common cause. This requires that they learn how to think longer-term, develop the art of persuasion, and have a broader view of the business. This is illustrated in Figure 1.2.

John Kotter, well-known Harvard professor and business consultant, has noted that moving from managing to leading requires a new way of thinking and behaving. In clinical practice terms, it means moving from seeing patients and entering orders to planning, collaborating, and

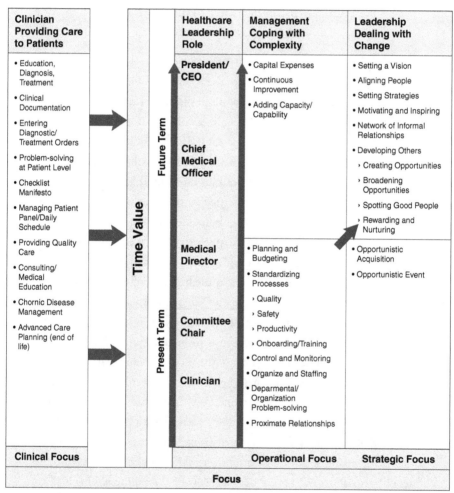

Figure 1.2 Migrating to leadership

motivating. In other words, it requires transitioning from short-term tactical behavior to longer-term strategic thinking and keeping broader organizational objectives in mind. It entails transforming from being the star player to being the team captain or the coach. Applying Kotter's model to health care and physician-leadership, a clinician managing patient care (the myriad of issues and decisions that surround physician–patient interactions) must evolve to coping with the complexity of health care operations and processes as they move into management roles such as medical directors. As physicians continue to progress on the leadership path and become CMOs or CEOs, their focus must turn to strategy and change management. In the chapters to follow, you will learn the skills required to make the transition from clinician to leader, learning new behaviors, while diminishing old, competing behaviors.

Managing Relationships: From Authority to Influence

In a clinical environment, relationships are focused on healing or ameliorating the symptoms of the patient. While it may sometimes feel to physicians that they spend most of the day convincing and cajoling patients, insurance companies, and health systems to follow their recommendations, the physician is still the primary authority in the clinical setting. The roles are clear, and all involved look to the physician for direction and commands.

However, in a physician-leadership role, it is not the physician that is the center of the decision-making universe. Rather, the focus is the function or organization that the physician serves. The physician-leadership role is further complicated when a physician has to manage other physicians in addition to nonphysicians. In these larger roles, where they are managing other physicians that were once peers, the command and control style so effective in the clinical setting is likely to be met with great resistance in a leadership role. Physicians, like all people, by nature, do not like to be managed. A natural consequence of the physician's training and the historical functioning of the clinical health system is the expectation that the physician's judgment should rarely be questioned.

When moving into a physician-leadership role, the new leader must learn a different way of dealing with others. The leader's role is one of using influence over authority, in order to get compliance or cooperation in service to the benefit of the overall organization. This role is much more nuanced and subtler than giving orders. The misconceptions of how much power or authority accompanies a title or position is one of the first issues new physician-leaders need to address. In a leadership role, the leader is on much more of a collegial level with whomever they lead than one might expect. Accomplishing major organizational initiatives requires the full cooperation and the greater resources of a team. In subsequent chapters, you will learn how to use influence over authority in creating a high-performing team.

Setting the Vision: From Microscope to Telescope

By design, the practice of the clinician is one that focuses primarily on short-term solutions, especially in the acute care setting. Although physicians are observant of longer-term problems, such as the sequelae of chronic medical conditions and end-of-life considerations, their practice predominantly focuses on the here and now. In referring back to Figure 1.2, the far-left column shows that physicians tend to spend their time and focus on short-term tactical issues.

The practice of medicine is one that is deep and narrow. This is especially true in the era of increasing medical subspecialization. This tapering scope of practice, coupled with the focus on detail and task orientation that is required to produce the best patient outcomes, actually hinders clinicians from thinking more comprehensively and seeing the broader landscape as they transition to leadership.

Although there is complexity with respect to all the considerations involved in making clinical decisions, physicians generally tend to see presenting problems with which they have become familiar and have, or can develop, a standard and consistent protocol. Evidence-based medicine is founded on the use of best practices that have been scientifically demonstrated to be effective. Of course, innovation is required to create new ideas, but the vast majority of physicians spend their days applying the evidence base as opposed to creating it.

However, in a leadership role, the leader is required to think much more strategically, considering implications for the function, organization, or system. The leader is required to think further ahead and identify possible challenges and opportunities that can impact both the organization and those who work in the organization, both clinicians and nonclinicians. No longer can the focus of attention be solely on the interaction with the patient. A physician-leader has to balance the needs of patients and the sometimes competing challenges of payers with those of the organization. Thus, these leaders need to consider innovative and untried ways to change and transform the enterprise.

The physician-leader must learn to embrace the upper right-hand quadrant of Figure 1.2, the strategic and longer-term. This focus includes major issues such as program development, evolving clinically through new models of care, the identification of new trends in treatment modalities and technology, and considerations of the implications of payer and patient mix. In addition to these business and medical considerations, the physician-leader needs to think about setting a vision, talent acquisition and development, succession planning, and how to inspire for maximum productivity and profitability.

Creating a High-Performing Team

The concept of a team for physician-leaders is vastly different from that of the physician in practice. Particularly in the acute care setting where shift work is the norm for many members of the health care team, physicians are often working with constantly changing teams and have little input in the selection of team members. In such environments, there is a predetermined group of health care professionals who have narrowly defined roles and clear expectations. They are a team in the sense that they all work together for a common solution under the direction of the physician for the relatively narrow patient issues usually presented. The "team-ness" of the group only exists in the presence of the patient and in reaching the prescribed conclusion. Duties are segregated, and the physician delegates tasks to other members of the health care team. However, this delegation exists primarily to facilitate task completion as opposed to development of new skills or succession planning. This tends to be a hub-and-spoke approach to leadership, with the physician being the hub, giving orders to those on the spokes (Figure 1.3).

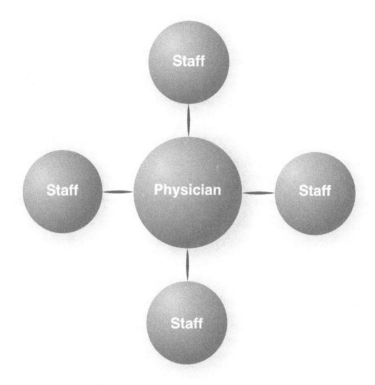

Figure 1.3 Hub-and-spoke leadership

The physician-leader is faced with a similar structure applied to a much bigger scope, with the added requirement that those on the team have much broader roles than in the operating room or clinical practice. Having a clear vision or charter for the physician-led team is critical for the success of the team, and subsequently the organization. However, the constitution of the team is one of fellow physicians, nursing leaders, nurses, and, in many cases, administrative professionals. The physician-leaders must change their model from that of hub-and-spokes to one of more equal collaboration (Figure 1.4). Delegation must occur to both complete tasks and to develop team members (see Chapter 7). Because they are in a leadership position, they will have some latitude in the selection of their team members and the qualifications required to address the current and future needs of the organization. The time frame is much longer, and the problems the team will face can be more complex, unique, and unfamiliar (see Chapter 6).

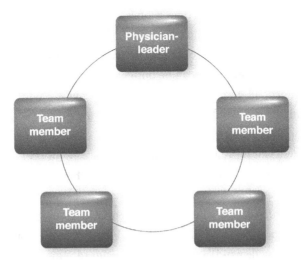

Figure 1.4 Collaborative leadership model

In the clinical setting, all team members are aligned to create the best possible outcomes for their patients. From the perspective of the clinical physician, this is the premise on which they function, and there is seemingly control over little else. The physician-leader will need to factor in team incentives that include remuneration, quality, patient care, and intangible rewards like doing the right thing for the organization. The physician-leader will lead the team members in establishing goals and aligning them with the vision, while creating processes for executing on goals that include ownership, time frames, accountabilities, rewards, and recognition. These physician-leaders and their teams will face multifaceted issues that, at times, compete with one another, such as managing cost while maintaining quality, meeting expectations with limited resources, holding team members accountable without alienating them. These complicated and challenging issues can be daunting for physicians transitioning into leadership. Fortunately, in the chapter on effective team building, you will find the kind of processes and structure required to create a high-performing team in the face of difficult challenges.

Communication and Negotiation

The reality of clinical practice requires communication to be quick, concise, and typically one-way. Even when not making life-or-death decisions, the role and expectation of "the doctor knows best" requires a type of communication that does not invite extensive dialogue. Most cases that physicians manage are routine and do not need a great deal of analysis or discussion to determine both an accurate diagnosis and treatment regimen. In addition, the pressure physicians are under to see as many patients as possible, without compromising quality, adds another dimension to brief, top-down communication.

As physicians move into leadership roles, the kind of communication they are required to have changes. Relationships change as the physician transitions from being a solo decision maker to being a leader having a team of professionals who often see themselves as peers and want to have input into major decisions. Those whom the leader now manages prefer, and may demand, to have their voices heard. This is a far different set of dynamics than in an operating room, hospital ward, or outpatient clinic. In addition, the issues faced by the physician-leader are very often unfamiliar and complex, requiring discussion with others to make the best decisions or find the best solutions. If physician-leaders maintain the same kind of unilateral communication that they employed in their practices, they run the risk of alienating their new teams and, ultimately, suboptimizing their roles or even failing.

Physician-leaders will also face a very different level of expectation with respect to managing others. In response to the top-down, authoritative (and sometimes authoritarian) communication in their practices, employees or ancillary staff typically follow orders and comply. In these circumstances, those who do not acquiesce tend to self-select out, considerably reducing the need for having difficult conversations.

However, the leader-led team is expected to be collaborative and to contribute to problem-solving initiatives. As a result, the physician-leader will often face challenges from those on the team who, by virtue of their positions, have a right, and even an obligation, to speak up. Learning how to conduct these difficult conversations is a new challenge for physicians, who, in their practices, have been the sole expert. The successful physician-leaders will be required to adapt their styles to include discussion, debate, and disagreement, in order to arrive at the best possible solution for the team, function, or organization. The constituents are varied, and the expectations differ greatly from those in their prior role.

When there are performance discussions, the effective physician-leader will want to understand when and how to intervene, the best approach to take, and how to create outcomes that are beneficial to the individual, the team, and the organization. This requires learning a process to have difficult conversations so that when a situation demands it, the physician-leader is prepared to have the discussion in a timely manner and with a positive outcome in mind. These difficult discussions require a very different approach than those for which the physicians' practice has prepared them. We provide tips, tools, and a process for the physician-leader to have a positive outcome for such difficult conversations (see Chapter 8).

Another type of difficult conversation comes in the form of negotiation. Physicians are frequently interested in how to sharpen their negotiation skills. In fact, as clinicians rise to more formal leadership positions, the ability to effectively negotiate becomes critical to their success. Too often, negotiation is thought of as a win–lose situation in which one person is trying to get the best deal either at the expense of, or at least without regard to, the other person. Think about your last car-buying experience! These adversarial dealings can be stressful and can end in suboptimal outcomes. We present a negotiation context that considers *both* the value of the outcome with the value of the relationship. When negotiation is done within this context, the possibility of having an outcome that is mutually beneficial is heightened. We provide you with tools to help in these situations. We are also aware that in some difficult negotiations, the most desirable outcomes cannot be achieved. We provide you with a proven method, and tools, to know when to walk away from difficult negotiations. Look in Chapter 9 for these tools.

Physician, Heal Thyself: Looking in the Mirror

Moving from being a physician to being a physician-leader is not an easy path. Here is why. Most physicians struggle while moving from clinical roles to administrative roles, from short-term to long-term thinking, from operating as solo decision maker to shared decision making, from giving orders to collaboration. In fact, all of the training of physicians has charged them with having ownership of, and responsibility for, patient health and outcomes. The very nature of this training is essential for developing effective clinicians but can be very detrimental to the development of physician-leaders.

Research on those who go into medicine has found that personality traits such as competitiveness, perfectionism, and even, at times, obsessive-compulsive behavior are common physician traits (Lipsenthal 2005). Other physician personality traits that can be detrimental in leadership positions include risk-aversion, safety-seeking, and difficulty finding a safe place to discuss stresses associated with their jobs. Physicians moving into leadership roles find challenges that include planning and organizing, the need for highly developed emotional intelligence, adaptability, managing change, conflict management, and holding others accountable (Warren 2017).

In short, moving from the physician role to that of physician-leadership is a big jump. In fact, it is jumping two levels at once. Typically, leadership roles are filled with people who have aspired to being in them and who have prepared by being in previous leadership roles. Usually, their education and career paths have aligned with moving into leadership positions. However, the expectation of the physician's training has focused on moving into a clinical role for their entire career.

Sometimes, physicians seek leadership roles to escape the pressures and ongoing difficulties associated with clinical practice. In this sense, they are "moving from" rather than "moving to." The weight of the many challenges they face is the driving force. Increasing workload, constant time pressures, chaotic work environments, declining pay, and endless bureaucratic tasks required by health insurance companies contribute to physician burnout. It is often this burnout that causes physicians to consider moving from clinical practice into leadership positions (Grinspoon 2018).

We believe that when physicians begin to consider moving into leadership positions, they should ask themselves why they want such a change. Are they "running away" or "running to?" If they are running away, particularly if they still enjoy working with patients, have they considered all of the possible solutions to address the issues that interfere with their clinical work? Have they sought out the advice of colleagues, mentors, or therapists?

If they are "running to," have they considered the many changes they will have to make in order to become effective leaders, such as developing business acumen, changing their communication and leadership styles, becoming collaborators and not simply order-givers, developing additional interpersonal skills, dealing with a completely different set of problems than they have found in clinical practice? We believe that before physicians move into leadership roles, even temporarily, a thorough self-examination will help them come to terms with why they are leaving clinical practices and to be realistic about the challenges ahead in a leadership role (see Chapter 3).

In spite of all these challenges, physicians *can* successfully transition into physician-leaders, and we believe that physician-leaders are the future of successful health care systems. By understanding and facing these challenges head-on, effective physician-leaders will be able to harvest the synergy created by combining clinical acumen and experience with administrative leadership skills. We hope that the observations and tactics contained in this book prove useful to you.

Coach's Corner

Moving from being a clinician to being a physician-leader is a huge step. In this chapter, we have introduced you to some of the challenges inherent in that transition. For physicians to make this transition, they must realize that their thinking, behavior, and way of interacting will have to undergo modification and change. Here are some considerations for making the transition.

1. **Internal motivation for change**
   - Physicians must truly understand why they want to move into physician-leadership. Are they "running away" from clinical practice or "running to" physician-leadership? Some combination of both driving forces is often at play, and a successful transition plan requires a personal understanding of this balance.

2. **Identify your strengths**
   - Clinicians bring unique and valuable perspectives and skills to leadership positions. Recognizing precisely what perspectives and skills will be most productive in leadership is essential so that emphasis can be placed on preserving these while developing new skills.

3. **Identify your opportunities**
   - New perspectives and skills are required as physicians transition to leadership positions. Although some of these opportunities will be identified during the transition and through the use of external resources, such as this book, there is incredible value in introspecting and in personally identifying developmental needs.

References

Grinspoon, P. June, 2018. "Physician Burnout Can Affect Your Health." *Harvard Health Publishing, Harvard Medical School.* https://www .health.harvard.edu/blog/physician-burnout-can-affect-your-health-2018062214093 (accessed September 15, 2018).

Lipsenthal, L. Fall, 2005. "The Physician Personality: Confronting Our Perfectionism and Social Isolation." *Holistic Primary Care* 6, no. 3. https://www.holisticprimarycare.net/topics/topics-o-z/reflections/200-the-physician-personality-confronting-our-perfectionism-and-social-isolation.html (accessed September 15, 2018).

Price, G., and T. Norbeck. September, 2017. "Physician-Leaders Will Shape the Future of Medicine." *Forbes.com.* https://www.forbes .com/sites/physiciansfoundation/2017/09/06/physician-leaders-will-shape-the-future-of-medicine/#18a2c2012766 (accessed September 8, 2018).

Warren, B. March, 2017. "Top Physician Personality Strengths and Challenges." *Healthcare Hiring Perspective Blog.* http://www .selectinternational.com/healthcare-hiring-blog/physician-personality-strengths-challenges (accessed September 15, 2018).

CHAPTER 2

The Business of Health Care

At no time in the history of our country has the business of health care been more hotly debated, or more divisive, than it is today. Progressives believe that, like education, everyone should have access to affordable health care. Some extremists believe that health care should be provided entirely by the government and not be an enterprise from which a profit should be generated, whereas others are just as adamantly invested in holding on to their private health care insurance. Putting health care in the same marketplace as automobiles, iPhones, or Starbucks is anathema to many. Some hope to see "Medicare for all," whereas others view it as a move toward socialism. The result is that health care leaders feel whipsawed, not knowing what direction will prevail and having difficulty making long-term decisions or knowing just where to place resources. Indeed, the health care business model is in flux as never before. The focus of this chapter is not to endorse a point of view, but to inform physician-leaders of business issues emerging in health care that they will need to be aware of and, ultimately, decide on.

Business Models and Health Care

The concept of profit in health care can have a negative connotation for many people, especially clinicians. However, generating a profit margin is essential for almost all health care organizations, including nonprofit health systems and academic medical centers. Nonprofit health systems must make money to fund initiatives such as charity care. Academic medical centers must fund education and research. A common adage among nonprofit health care leaders is "no margin, no mission." As you can see, profit generation in health care is just as important as it is in other businesses. The utilization of that profit is what differentiates one health care organization from the next.

Every business, health care included, has as its foundation a business model. A business model includes products or services, resources, processes, distribution, and end users. Every business model has a value proposition answering two questions. First, "how will we make money in this business?" and, secondly, "why will customers or end users choose our products and services over those of the competition?" In market-driven businesses, the business model is how a company will generate revenue and make a profit. Typical business models look like this one of Mercedes (Figure 2.1).

Company	Products	End-use customers	Logistics	Distribution	Awareness	Value proposition
Mercedes-Benz	Premium vehicles	Affluent drivers wanting a world-class luxury experience	German engineering through R&D to manufacturer to select dealers to affluent customers	Independent select dealers worldwide	Advertising to affluent customer candidates through both mass media and luxury venues	German engineering with an international flair that meets the needs, demands, and desires of luxury buyers around the world

Figure 2.1 Mercedes business model

In this business model, Mercedes seeks to differentiate itself from competitors in terms of the buyer to which it markets (affluent) and the value it offers those customers (German engineering, international flair, luxury). Mercedes unashamedly focuses on a narrow and select consumer base, for which it charges a premium price for the privilege of being a member of an elite driving group. Much of the appeal of driving a Mercedes is the heightened perception others will have of you for being able to drive such a fine and expensive car. In fact, the Mercedes tagline is "The Best or Nothing." This differentiator is evident throughout their business model.

Applying this business model template to a health care organization may feel a bit awkward at first. This is exactly why the exercise brings value. The business perspective is only one of many perspectives in health care, but ignoring this perspective will limit health care leaders as they strive to bring success to their organizations. In Figure 2.2, we illustrate how the fictitious XYZ Cancer Center would describe the business model of its organization.

Company	Products	End-use customers	Logistics	Distribution	Awareness	Value proposition
XZY Cancer Center	State-of-the art cancer treatment	Informed cancer patients desiring the most up-to-date treatment options	Laboratory and clinical research translated to bedside by highly trained oncologists delivering care to cancer patients	Flagship cancer center with multi-state spoke facilities augmented by telemedicine services	Advertising to cancer patients and their families through direct-to-consumer mass media and outreach to referring physicians	Best-in-class cancer care that offers both standard care of common cancers and advanced, research-based treatment when needed

Figure 2.2 XYZ Cancer Center business model

Every health care organization should consider and define its business model as Mercedes and XYZ Cancer Center have in order to facilitate its success. Similarly, to properly steer their organizations, physician-leaders should seek to understand and refine their organization's business model. This may be easier said than done for new physician-leaders. Clinical physicians have a wealth of knowledge about the diagnosis and treatment of patients. However, they sometimes lack perspective surrounding the actual delivery of health care in areas such as operational logistics and costs of care. In the transition from clinician to leader, it is crucial that physicians can recognize the big picture as leading health care organizations requires balancing the desired diagnostic and treatment options with operational capabilities and costs to the system. This is not an option but rather a requirement in this age of increasingly finite resources. Although some of this perspective can be obtained through various educational programs, much of this insight is the result of experience and on-the-job training.

As a foundation, physician-leaders need to understand the broader landscape of health care. The traditional business model of the U.S. health care system is fee for service, providing discrete payments for each health care service delivered. This incentivizes quantity of care with relative disregard for quality of care. No doubt, most clinicians within the system have striven to deliver only the best care possible to their patients, but one cannot ignore the underlying financial incentives.

We are in the midst of a transition in health care from fee for service reimbursement to value-based reimbursement. Value-based reimbursement includes tactics such as pay-for-performance incentives, penalties for adverse events such as hospital acquired conditions or readmissions, and population health management using tools such as preventive care and lifestyle modification to reduce health care utilization. This transition has been rumored for decades, yet the actual change process has been extremely gradual. It is impossible to predict when the U.S. health care system will actually be more value-based than fee for service, but this eventuality is appearing to be more and more likely. At the very least, the last few years have seen an acceleration in value-based reimbursement, led by the Centers for Medicare and Medicaid Services, with commercial payors quickly following suit. The successful physician-leader will prepare his or her organization with the knowledge and skills necessary to thrive in a value-based system when necessary.

There is another important transition that is occurring in health care. Like it or not, the traditional professional-centered health care model is in the process of evolving into a new, patient-centered model. Increased focus on patient experience is but one example of this change. Another example is recent legislation requiring hospitals and providers to post the costs of their services. As seen in Figure 2.3, the changes impact virtually all aspects of the health care business model (Giesen 2013).

From: Traditional healthcare	To: New healthcare model
• Professional centered	• Patient-centered
• Effectiveness & efficiency	• Value
• Opinion-based	• Evidence-based
• Event	• Pathway
• Organization	• Network
• Structure	• System
• Clinical practice peripheral	• Clinical practice central
• Money-driven	• Knowledge-driven

Figure 2.3 Changing health care model

Source: Giesen (2013).

Health care consumerism is a term that has been thrown about for many years. Understanding health care consumerism means understanding that the business of health care is fundamentally different from most market-based businesses. Patients are challenged to effectively exercise consumer choice as it is very difficult for them to accurately assess the quality of health care services. How can a patient without any medical education understand the potential treatment options available and the possible outcomes of any disease process? Additionally, because each patient's health profile is relatively unique, it is impossible for them to compare their own situation with that of friends and family members. Despite this, increased transparency of cost and quality in health care along with easily accessible information on the Internet is slowly but surely advancing the practice of health care consumerism.

The U.S. health care system fosters significant innovation in the clinical practice arena, with constant research occurring on new diagnostic and treatment modalities. However, the business and operations of health care have lagged significantly behind other industries in creating innovative practices and tools that could lead to better patient care. Is there any practicing clinician who has not wondered why the practice of medicine is so complex, inefficient, and difficult? As a result, consumers suffer with less-than-optimal products, high costs, and inefficiencies across the value chain. These health care issues include (Hoban, Michelson, and Stone 2017):

- Increased costs without demonstrably better outcomes
- Opaque and inconsistent pricing, making it difficult to assess the value of the product
- Complex and confusing interactions with health care systems
- Painfully slow, and expensive, product evolution with little innovation
- Generic offerings that try to serve everyone and thus serve no one well

Unlike other industries that have embraced innovation and customer-centric business models, health care is, by far, a laggard. The advent of big data, technology, and customer focus has transformed industries in hospitality, transportation, and, especially, retail (e.g. Amazon). Being able to harness existing data to impact clinical diagnoses and outcomes will change the future of health care. Big data and analytics along with research in health care advancements and technology platforms will improve patient outcomes, reduce unnecessary patient visits, and make access to health care easier for consumers. Technology is creating a more informed health care consumer with greater choice and access. In addition to easily accessible online medical information, social media platforms are impacting consumer opinion. As with other industries, health care consumers want convenience, greater choice, more discretionary time (i.e., not in clinical settings), and have an increased interest in health and wellness. These trends also will continue to drive changes, and even transform, the health care business model (Hoban, Michelson, and Stone 2017).

There is no question that change is coming. Physician-leaders need to understand the current forces in health care that impact health care operations in addition to patient interactions and motivations. Those physician-leaders that are able to become agile, learn quickly, embrace new technology wisely, and adapt will fare much better than those who are loyally entrenched in the system as it has been. Those physician-leaders who think and act boldly and differently are much more likely to be successful than those who persistently defend the status quo. What a great opportunity for physicians to take leading roles in this transformative time!

Value Disciplines in Business

There are some notable health care structures that have emerged with which physician-leaders will need to become well versed as they move into positions of influence and strategic decision making. We will look at some potential value-based structures and consider how they might work in this new health care environment. It has been known for years that businesses can be characterized by the disciplines to which they subscribe. These are the disciplines that successful companies employ. They are called "value disciplines" and include best cost, best product, or best solution. Successful companies must be proficient in at least one of these disciplines while maintaining acceptable standards in the other two. The disciplines are as follows (Treacy and Wiersema 1997):

- Operational Excellence: The ability of a company or organization to provide low-cost products and services, dependability, or convenience.
- Product Leadership: Companies that regularly bring new, high-performing, and valued products to market, usually at premium prices.
- Customer Intimacy: A focus on close relationships with their customers as well as best overall solutions, often at premium prices.

When considering the value-based transformation taking place in health care, these disciplines differentiate one health care organization from another. The following are examples of hospitals and health care systems that have excelled in changing the traditional health care model.

Operational Excellence: Hospitals and systems that focus on operational excellence will also focus on waste management and waste reduction. Health care is notorious for managing waste poorly and creating excess costs. The tremendous waste and inefficiency in health care has been documented in publications like the *New York Times* and *Time* magazine. This contributes to the unacceptably high costs of health care. The cost of health care in the United States is nearly double that of its peer countries and without much better outcomes (Sanger-Katz 2018). Despite the aforementioned difficulties of health care consumerism, there are legions of patients that will shop around for the lowest-cost health care as long as quality is not sacrificed. Health care systems that emphasize value through scale and scope will find success by focusing on operational efficiency.

Intermountain Health in Utah is an example of this model. It has partnered with six other systems to form a nonprofit generic drug company to reduce hospital drug costs and prevent drug shortages. By controlling more of the value stream, Intermountain Health is able to lower the cost of drugs to their patients (LaPointe 2018). Intermountain Health has also invested in other cost lowering initiatives like telehealth in a variety of settings. Achieving lower treatment and medication costs yet maintaining high levels of quality is not an easy task. It is one that takes commitment from every part of the hospital system and requires change management, including buy-in from physicians. It is one way to transform the current health care model. The physician-leader is particularly well situated to influence physician peers in considering how such changes will result in a better long-term solution for them and the system.

Product Leadership: Innovation is often sacrificed at the altar of cost management. Health care organizations that invest in innovation make these investments with the hope that they will see a return timely enough to satisfy critics and justify the investment. Advances in technology have been at the foundation of these innovations. Technology innovations have come in two categories—processes and products.

With electronic medical record (EMR) systems, there are mountains of data available that have the potential to change the course of treatment. However, unlocking the big data and translating it into tangible benefits has been elusive. Currently, physicians have access to significant amounts of data that is poorly processed and difficult to understand or analyze. This data is a far cry from being information. By harnessing the data available from EMRs and other data systems to create actionable business intelligence, physicians and other leaders can be empowered to drive positive change.

A second example of using big data more effectively is the application of predictive analytics. By using predictive analytics in health care, hospitals and physicians can "get ahead" of problems, support population health management, and get better outcomes across the continuum of care. Hospitals and health systems that have taken the next step in predictive analytics are able to become more adept at risk scoring for chronic diseases, avoid 30-day hospital readmissions, prevent suicide and self-harm, better manage the supply chain to reduce costs and unnecessary spending, and ensure stronger data security (Bresnick 2018).

With regard to product innovation, hospitals that specialize, or invest in specialized service lines, are better suited to capitalize on technological advancement. An example is the use of artificial intelligence in diagnosis. Researchers have demonstrated that a form of artificial intelligence, the convolutional neural network (CNN), is better than experienced dermatologists at detecting skin cancer (Haenssle et al. 2018). This research has been replicated and expanded to eight skin diseases. Imagine the benefits of increased detection through artificial intelligence. Once initial invest- ment costs are recovered, the ongoing costs would be reduced, requiring fewer ancillary staff.

El Camino Hospital cancer center has adopted CyberKnife as a pain- less alternative to traditional radiation therapy or surgery. Surgeons are able to remove tumors in about 90 percent of cases. Because the treat- ment is noninvasive, it is particularly valuable for sensitive areas. In ad- dition, it does not require anesthesia, allowing patients a remarkably fast recovery time and increased chances of success (UIC, n.d.).

Hospitals and health care systems that focus on innovation understand that they must do things differently. Innovation and product leadership is not about a "one and done" or "the next shiny object," nor is it sim- ply about continuous improvement. Continuous improvement should be foundational to the culture of any health care enterprise. Health care systems that embrace innovation understand that they need to have a long-term view of their investment dollars. Innovation requires invest- ment, and these systems must have ample funds to sustain the bets they are placing and be patient. Innovation is not a short-term fix. In addition, health care leaders understand that not all of their innovation expendi- tures will return a profit. However, like the examples we cited, innovation should result in work becoming easier, patient outcomes improving, and benefits outweighing the cost of not having done anything innovative at all (Gamble 2013).

Customer Intimacy: Hospitals and health care systems that shift from "one size fits all" medicine to treating every patient and their prob- lems uniquely will be at the forefront of customer intimacy. Most medical treatments are designed with the average person in mind. The problem is that no one is average. Every patient is unique with idiosyncrasies that can make the average treatments suboptimal. In 2016, President Obama launched the Precision Medicine Initiative with a $200-million invest- ment for research. According to the National Institute of Health, precision medicine is "an emerging approach for disease treatment and prevention that takes into account individual variability in genes, environment, and lifestyle for each person."

Precision health considers genetics; genetic testing; patient responses to medication; where a patient works, lives; what they eat; hobbies; etc. The goal is to understand how all of these determinants affect their health risk and health goals. According to Megan Mahoney, MD, Chief of General Primary Care, Division of Primary Care and Population Health at Stanford University, the focus is on using scientific research and genetic testing advances to predict what diseases will most likely occur in patients, individualize interventions, and even prevent diseases before they strike. The goal is to "predict, prevent and cure precisely" (Jakucs 2019).

This approach to medicine is individualized and customized. It focuses on prevention and early, targeted intervention. It is the ultimate in driving up quality and driving down costs because of the focus on disease prevention and early treatment. Precision health represents the shift from the traditional professional-centered model to the new patient-centered model of medicine. Focusing on prevention, rather than solely on cure or amelioration, places the healthy patient, rather than the physician, at the center of the interaction. Hospitals are quickly moving into the precision health area, including Stanford, UCLA Health, University of Michigan, and the University of Chicago.

One of the main problems with precision health is the payoff. After all of the early revenue is captured from the initial assessment, lifestyle interviews, and genetic testing, the precision health model has a payoff that can be difficult to capture. Because the focus is on disease prevention and early treatment, precision health will drive up quality and lower costs for the patient. In effect, hospitals and health care systems are looking for ways to get rewarded for something that *didn't* happen. In the future of value-based reimbursement, this approach will provide significant rewards to health care facilities and providers. Conversely, to change someone's habits and lifestyle so that they can push the onset of any disease further into the future can cause revenue shortages in the meantime.

Another approach to the transformation of medicine through customer intimacy is concierge medicine. Concierge medicine is a system in which patients pay an additional fee for more personalized, and presumably better, access to their doctors. The current focus on volume in health care means that patients see their physicians only periodically, more often having their treatment delegated to a nurse practitioner or physician assistant. For patients that have the financial resources, want to have more personalized care, and desire to see their physician instead of being passed off, concierge medicine is an option. Essentially, the physician is put on a retainer for this highly personalized service. The benefit for physicians is that they are able to see fewer patients and still continue to make a good living. In fact, according to MedScape's 2017 Physician Compensation Report, physicians who use the concierge model of payment make about two percent more than the average earnings of all physicians while seeing dramatically fewer patients (Hedges 2019).

Because concierge medicine is an emerging field, there are a number of issues that will need to be addressed for it to become mainstream. In an environment where there is currently a drastic shortfall in the number of physicians, estimated to be between 60,000 to 90,000 by 2025 (according to the Association of American Medical Colleges), concierge medicine further reduces the number of physicians available for patient care. Secondly, because the cost of concierge medicine is so high, it drastically reduces the pool of people who might benefit from the services. Only those individuals with significant resources can afford the very high cost of these services. Insurance companies do not pay for concierge services at this time; the fee is paid out of pocket by the patient. This further reduces access for the vast majority of the population. The American Academy of Family Physicians does not support concierge medicine, believing that it could reduce the number of patients with access to primary care. Finally, physicians who elect to change their practices to the concierge model will need to become more adept at marketing in order to be successful. The concierge physician will need to act more like an entrepreneur than one working for a hospital or health care system.

There are a select number of hospitals that are adding concierge medicine to their services. Among them are Mayo Clinic, Stanford Health Care, Duke Health, Massachusetts General Hospital, and Virginia Mason

Health System. These hospitals provide patients who have chronic conditions or busy schedules with the ability to schedule same-day appointments or text a doctor day and night if health issues arise. The annual retainer ranges from $2,500 to $6,000 (Livingston 2017). These fees are above and beyond the charges billed to insurance companies. These hospitals often have physicians that are salaried, so the financial margin from the concierge medicine practice goes to support the mission of the greater entity. The practice of concierge medicine is still evolving, but the demand for these kinds of services seems to be increasing and receiving more acceptance from reputable institutions.

Health Care Metrics: What Physician-Leaders Need to Know

As physician-leaders move into positions in which they are influencing major hospital and system decisions, it is crucial that they understand metrics and the data of which they are composed. In health care as in other industries, the mantra that "we manage what we measure" has never been more true.

Health care metrics encompass three broad categories: quality, operational, and financial. Physician-leaders will likely be following metrics in all of these categories. There are a number of factors that need to be considered in association with these metrics. The first step is to identify the metrics that are most important to your particular organization. These are your organization's key performance indicators (KPIs). Some organizations have 10 KPIs and some have 30 KPIs, but it is always important to limit your KPIs to only the most important metrics. Selecting too many metrics as KPIs can create distractions as opposed to creating focus, as KPIs should. You know you have identified the correct KPIs if they encompass exactly the data necessary to tell you whether your organization is succeeding or failing.

Once the KPIs have been selected, it is essential to define each metric. This means specifying the source of the data, the owner of the data, and defining the exact details of each metric. For example, the septic shock mortality rate could be defined as the number of deaths in people with septic shock on their hospital diagnosis list divided by the total number of people with septic shock on their hospital diagnosis list during the same period. Further, the source of this data is the hospital's clinical data warehouse, and the owner is the director of quality. This exercise ensures that everyone in the organization is speaking the same language and partaking in the same data when examining the metrics of the organization. Many organizations speak of a "single source of truth" in relation to data. Although having a single, comprehensive source of data is aspirational, the process of defining metrics accomplishes the goal of avoiding data confusion and debate in the same manner regardless of how many data sources are being used.

For most metrics, especially quality metrics, consideration should be given to whether a balancing measure should also be tracked. Use of balancing metrics allows leaders to understand whether the pursuit of performance in one area is suboptimizing another. One common example is tracking readmission rates as a balancing measure to length of stay. Many hospitals have the goal of reducing length of stay for hospitalized patients. However, when length of stay is driven too low, readmission rates begin to rise. Only by tracking both metrics can hospital leaders know when they have successfully focused on reducing length of stay while not sacrificing readmission rates.

Finally, it is imperative that each leader determines the frequency at which each metric should be reviewed. Depending on the specifics of each organization, metrics must be reviewed daily, weekly, monthly, quarterly, or even annually. Figure 2.4 shows what noted health care leader, Quint Studer, considers the appropriate frequency for following what he considers the KPIs of any hospital. Some of you may not remember that he was once a successful hospital CEO before he became the guru of patient experience.

Health care is changing rapidly. Physicians, when moving from clinician to leader, will need to broaden their scope so that they are in positions in which they make changes and do not simply repeat the status quo. As they consider the structure of the organizations they serve, they will want to understand the need for their institutions to move from traditional models of medicine to those that are more transformational and value-based. By being adept at understanding business models and business foci options, physician-leaders can become thought leaders and change agents in their systems.

Indicator	Daily	Monthly	Quarterly	Annually
Productivity/volume				
Patient volumes	X	X		
Outpatient no-shows	X	X		
ER wait times	X	X		
ER departure times	X	X		
ER vacating patients	X	X		
Average hospital stay		X		
Readmission rates		X		
Patient experience				
Patient satisfaction		X	X	X
Patient safety	X			X
Quality metrics		X		
Staff Experience				
Staff turnover		X		
Agency usage		X		
Staff issues	X			
Staff evaluations			X	X
Revenue Considerations				
Total operating margin		X		
Days cash on hand		X	X	X
Claims denial rate		X		
Bad debt		X		
AR days outstanding		X		
Agency and overtime		X		
Treatment costs			X	

Figure 2.4 Hospital leader dashboard

Source: Studer (2013) and Datapine (n.d.).

Coach's Corner

The business of health care integrates clinical, operational, and financial spheres. Physician-leaders must understand these concepts in general yet apply them specifically with consideration for the uniqueness of the organizations that they serve.

1. **Identify your organization's business model**
   - Using the template described in this chapter, outline your organization's business model. Is it well defined? Does it create market differentiation for the organization? Does it need to be further developed and refined?
2. **Reflect on the three value disciplines**
   - Scrutinize your organization's performance in relation to the three value disciplines (Operational Excellence, Product Leadership, Customer Intimacy). Is your organization competent in all three disciplines? Does it excel in at least one of these disciplines?
3. **Identify 5 KPIs**
   - Think about your organization and the factors that drive its success. Identify 5 KPIs as a foundation for creating your organization's comprehensive KPI dashboard.

References

Bresnick, J. September, 2018. "10 High-Value Use Cases for Predictive Analytics in Healthcare." *Health Analytics*. https://healthitanalytics.com/news/10-high-value-use-cases-for-predictive-analytics-in-healthcare (accessed February 28, 2019).

Datapine. n.d. "Healthcare Key Performance Indicators and Metrics." *datapine*. https://www.datapine.com/kpi-examples-and-templates/healthcare (accessed March 2, 2019).

Gamble, M. September, 2013. "5 Things the Most Innovative Health Systems Do Differently." *Becker's Hospital Review*. https://www.beckershospitalreview.com/hospital-management-administration/5-things-the-most-innovative-health-systems-do-differently.html (accessed February 28, 2019).

Giesen, D. 2013. "New Models in Healthcare Provision." *Conferencias saude cuf. Mobile Health: Novas Formas De Olhar A Saude*. https://www.slideshare.net/djegiesen/20130615-new-business-models-in-healthcare-provision-dgv10 (accessed February 20, 2019).

Haenssle, H.A., et al. May, 2018. "Man against Machine: Diagnostic Performance of a Deep Learning Convolutional Neural Network for Dermoscopic Melanoma Recognition in Comparison to 58 Dermatologists." *Annals of Oncology* 29, no. 1.

Hedges, L. 2019. "A Concierge Medicine Guide: Definition, Salary & Set-Up Info." *Healthy Practices*. https://www.softwareadvice.com/resources/concierge-medicine-salary-and-definition (accessed March 2, 2019).

Hoban, C., J. Michelson, and T. Stone. 2017. November, 2017. "Industry Interrupted Report: The Roadmap to Healthcare's Disruption." *Oliver Wyman Health*. https://www.oliverwyman.com/our-expertise/insights/2017/nov/health-innovation-journal/industry-disrupted/special-report--industry-interrupted.html (accessed February 26, 2019).

Jakucs, C. 2019. "Precision Health Is the Wave of the Future." *Nurse.com*. https://resources.nurse.com/diversity-in-nursing-precision-health (accessed February 28, 2019).

LaPointe, J. September, 2018. "Hospitals Create Drug Company to Combat Drug Shortages, Prices." *Revcycle Intelligence*. https://revcycleintelligence.

com/news/hospitals-create-drug-company-to-combat-drug-shortages-prices (accessed February 27, 2019).

Livingston, S. October, 2017. "Concierge Care Taking Hold at Some Large, Urban Hospitals." *Modern Healthcare.* https://www.modern-healthcare.com/article/20171021/NEWS/171019863/concierge-care-taking-hold-at-some-large-urban-hospitals (accessed March 2, 2019).

Sanger-Katz, M. August, 2018. "How to Tame Health Care Spending? Look for One-Percent Solutions." *The New York Times.* https://www.nytimes.com/2018/08/27/upshot/rising-health-care-costs-economists-propose-small-solutions.html (accessed February 27, 2019).

Studer, Q. July, 2013. "The Hospital CEOs Ultimate Dashboard: What to Check Daily, Quarterly and Yearly." *Becker's Hospital Review.* https://www.beckershospitalreview.com/hospital-management-administration/the-hospital-ceo-s-ultimate-dashboard-what-to-check-daily-quarterly-and-yearly.html (accessed March 2, 2019).

Treacy, M., and F. Wiersema. 1997. *The Discipline of Market Leaders.* New York, NY: Addison-Wesley.

UIC. n.d. "6 Innovative Health Systems Implementing HIT." *University of Illinois at Chicago blog.* https://healthinformatics.uic.edu/blog/top-6-hospitals-using-health-technology (accessed February 28, 2019).

CHAPTER 3

The Psychology of the Physician-Leader: Genotype or Phenotype?

Are physicians made or born? Beyond simply being a question for debate, the answer to this question could have significant implications for future physicians and physician-leaders. We recently interviewed a hospital executive with degrees in business from an Ivy League school and an advanced degree from the London School of Economics. He had moved up through the ranks of hospital management from the nonclinical side rather than from the clinical side. When questioned about his career path, he volunteered that he wanted to go to medical school but performed poorly on the Medical College Admission Test (MCAT) after taking it several times.

He had concluded that he simply did not have the *genes* to be a physician, meaning that while he was clearly very bright, the *way* in which he thought and behaved was not conducive to becoming a physician. He was able to cite, in instance after instance, ways in which he approached problem-solving and decision making differently from those of physicians with whom he worked. Having worked in health care settings for a total of 40+ years, the authors have regularly seen these kinds of assertions, from both within and outside the ranks of physicians.

To better understand the psychology of the physician, we need to identify those behaviors and underlying characteristics that lend themselves to becoming a physician. The answer to the *nature-versus-nurture* debate has potential benefits for the selection of individuals for the medical field. At the intersection of science and its application is the understanding of genotype and phenotype.

You may remember that *genotype* is the heritable genetic identity an organism carries. Genotype determines whether an individual has blue eyes or brown, blonde hair or red, a disposition to diabetes or to alcoholism. Phenotypes are the *observable* part of an organism, influenced by both genotypes and the environment. An individual's tendency to gain weight, be anxious or calm, or like cats over dogs is at the confluence of their genotype and the environment in which they live.

When discussing personality, psychologists are referring to *individual differences* in characteristic patterns of thinking, feeling, and behaving. The study of personality involves identifying such individual differences as tendencies toward sociability or aloofness, irritability or calmness, emotional stability or lability, risk-taking or stasis-seeking. This process of understanding individual differences is used for identifying behaviors that contribute to mental illness; inclusion on the Olympic team; selection of a CEO; acting and singing opportunities, etc. In fact, identifying individual differences plays a very important role in our daily lives, including such issues as whom we trust, with whom we want to affiliate, the cars we drive, the political parties to which we belong, the foods we eat and why. The entirety of the selections and choices we make becomes our *observable* personality to the rest of the world. We become, and are identified by, these patterns of behavior that are a result of the choices we make, the habits we develop, and in some cases, our *genetic* predispositions.

By using the science of individual differences, we will be able to understand the psychology of the physician. We want to understand what *unique* individual characteristics lend themselves to actually becoming a physician. It is important to understand how physicians are different from the general population and how they are different from each other in the specialties they choose. In subsequent chapters, we will describe how the unique characteristics of physicians facilitate or hamper physicians in leadership roles. We will use a funnel approach as a method for understanding the psychology of the physician and how physicians are different from those in other occupations (Figure 3.1).

This approach will provide a clearer picture of what characteristics differentiate physicians from the general population and from their colleagues in different medical specialties. By understanding the individual differences of physicians, we can target the specific tools and capabilities

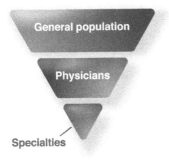

Figure 3.1 Funnel of individual differences

physicians will require in becoming physician-leaders. We begin our pursuit of understanding the psychology of the physician with an understanding of the origins of personality—nature or nurture?

Personality Theory and the Physician

The study of personality is the study of individual differences. The prevailing model used for understanding personality is the *Big Five Personality Factors*. From a meta-analysis of over 40 years of research studies on personality theory, psychologist John Digman was able to identify the key personality traits that contribute to personality (Digman 1990). These factors are described in Figure 3.2. This research has been foundational in refining personality theory and the science of individual differences. Each of these factors is broad enough to be inclusive of those characteristics that most contribute to an individual's personality. Several personality assessments have been created to capture these individual differences, including the Neuroticism–Extraversion–Openness Personality Inventory Revised Test (NEO PI-R) and the Hogan Personality Inventory (HPI) (Costa and McCrae 1992; Hogan and Hogan 2007). Using these measures, research results have helped identify those individual differences.

Assessments that measure the Big Five Personality Factors are looking for *traits* rather than *states*. For example, there are times when everyone experiences periods of anxiety. In fact, there are situations in which if some anxiety is not experienced, performance may actually decrease (e.g., an Olympic race). These situations are *states,* and the anxiety will

Personality domain	Definition	Facets
Neuroticism (emotional instability)	General tendency to experience negative effects (e.g., fear, embarrassment, anger) in response to stress	Anxious, depressed, self-conscious, impulsive, vulnerable, stress prone
Extraversion	General sociability with a cheerful disposition and strong interest in enterprising occupations	Assertive, energetic, gregarious, excitement-seeking
Openness to experience	General attentiveness to inner feelings, intellectual curiosity, and independence of judgment	Imaginative, creative, curious, open-minded, insightful
Agreeableness	A measure of interpersonal tendencies, assessing how an individual values different aspects of a relationship	compassionate, cooperative, collaborative, altruistic, trusting
Conscientiousness	Management of impulses and desires with predisposed investment in planning, organizing, and carrying out tasks	disciplined, dutiful, efficient, achievement-seeking, detail-oriented, risk-averse

Figure 3.2 Big Five Personality Factors

Source: Digman (1990).

recede when the precipitating event is over. However, when the same characteristic is present *in the absence of* a precipitating event and is persistent, the characteristic can be considered a more stable *trait* and less likely to change. In the general population, there would be a range of the expression of traits that would approximate a bell curve. As we proceed to understand the *traits* that comprise the personality of a physician, we will have a clearer view of those characteristics that differentiate physicians from the general population and their implications for becoming a physician-leader.

Personality and Genes: Nature

What aspects of personality are determined from birth? Much remains to be understood about how, what, and why personality traits are influenced. This is the realm of behavioral genetics and exists in the context of epidemiology, evolutionary psychology, and psychological domains. Research on twins has yielded the greatest data on this subject, and, apart from physical characteristics, results have been mixed.

According to twin studies, the Big Five Personality Factors have substantial heritable components explaining 40 to 60 percent of the variance. However, the identification of associated genetic variants has remained elusive. In the largest study to date, looking at heritability of each of the Big Five Personality Factors, some interesting results were found. Recent studies have found significant and substantial heritability estimates for neuroticism and openness, but not for extraversion, agreeableness or conscientiousness (Power and Pluess 2015). These findings suggest that issues such as emotional stability, psychopathology, and certain psychiatric disorders have a sizable genetic component. It is still the interaction between these genetic factors and the environment that contributes to specific behaviors being evident or managed. We will discuss these findings later in the chapter as they relate to physicians.

Personality and Environment: Nurture

It is the *interaction* of the genotype with the environment that begins to shape an individual's personality. The development of personality becomes increasingly shaped by the individual's family, socioeconomic factors, education, experiences in life, and so forth as the person grows. Although some things are, and will continue to be, fixed (e.g., eye color), other characteristics emerge as the dance between the individual and his or her environment becomes more complex and sophisticated.

Genes and Environment: Nature *and* Nurture

As we have known for many years, the question of nature versus nurture is not one of whether one or the other is the sole determining factor. The question of nature versus nurture revolves around the relative contributions of genetics and environment to the ultimate expression of an organism. Personality is clearly a combination of nature and nurture. Applied to physicians, which genetic tendencies predispose people to choose medicine as a career? Which tendencies are selected for in the medical school admission process? How are these genetic tendencies molded or shaped throughout medical training and practice to produce the personalities that we ultimately see in physicians?

Medical School: Selecting and Differentiating Physicians from the General Population

We can surmise that those who apply for medical school have a greater interest in the sciences, apply themselves well in their academic pursuits, are serious about their studies, and are more intelligent than the average university student. Most physicians would agree that admittance into medical school is dependent on how a prospective student performs on *The Big Three*:

- MCAT scores
- Undergraduate GPA
- Extracurricular activities (research, postgraduate coursework, volunteer commitments, etc.)

In other words, medical schools tend to focus more on academic performance and the *cognitive* domains for selection than on the *noncognitive* domains. By focusing only, or at least primarily, on academic performance, medical schools can underestimate the influence that noncognitive traits, such as being highly stress-prone, can have on student success.

Recently, the use of additional tools has augmented these traditional criteria for medical student selection at some medical schools. In particular, the Computer-Based Assessment for Sampling Personal Characteristics (CASPer) test assesses students' suitability for professions that require empathy and emotional maturity. However, to date, noncognitive assessments have had only minimal impact on medical student selection. It is reasonable to theorize that, at a minimum, the medical school selection process creates a subgroup of the general population that has higher intelligence and, from a personality perspective, is highly conscientious.

Once the selection of medical students occurs, we do know what it takes to succeed in medical school. In fact, research using the Big Five Personality Factors has found that medical students who are successful measure high in *conscientiousness, extraversion, and openness to experience.* On the other hand, *neuroticism* was a strong contraindicator for medical school success. Those individuals who are more likely to become emotionally upset were more at risk for having poor academic performance in medical school (Lievens, Ones, and Dilchert 2009; Ferguson et al. 2010).

Conscientiousness includes characteristics such as being dutiful, risk averse, persistent, responsible, and disciplined. Attention to detail and working with a sense of deliberation (versus a sense of urgency) also define this characteristic. The tendency to measure twice (or more) and cut once is drilled into the nascent medical student. No doubt, patients are grateful to have physicians who will take time to understand their symptoms and undertake a range of diagnostic tests prior to arriving at a final diagnosis. In the face of possible life and death decisions, the sense of responsibility that physicians shoulder is enormous and requires a heightened sense of conscientiousness.

Medical students high in *extraversion* and *openness to experience* were seen as struggling early in medical school, likely because their gregariousness interfered with their studies (and conscientiousness). However, once the threshold of classroom studies was crossed, extraverts actually performed very well with their patients. In addition, extraversion has been seen to be a generally positive characteristic in physicians in any number of postmedical school roles. Medical students were more likely to evidence extraversion than other university majors, including arts/humanities and psychology (Vedel 2016).

Similarly, possessing *openness to experience* became a greater indicator of academic success in the latter periods of study when applied practice becomes a greater part of the curriculum. The early aspects of medical school require a great deal of memorization and learning body systems, symptoms, diseases, and treatment. There is little time for questioning, and challenging professors is not encouraged. It is primarily in the applied part of the curriculum where being intellectually curious and creative becomes an asset (Lievens, Ones, and Dilchert 2009). It is during the interaction with patients that the investigative nature of the physician becomes more active. The need to think more broadly about a patient's symptoms and disease process requires the medical student to become more integrated in his or her thinking than the high degree of emphasis on memorizing and learning new material of the earlier years.

We begin to see a *pattern of behaviors* that is shaped in medical school and that distinguishes physicians from the general population. Of particular interest, the measure of these traits of conscientiousness, extraversion, and openness *increased* over the life of a medical student. Entering students' scores on these traits were lower than those of the *same* students in their later years of medical school. This finding is further recognition that medical school does, in fact, play a large role in the shaping of the personality of the physician by both selecting and reinforcing certain personality traits.

The Personality of the Physician

In one of the largest studies comparing physicians with the general population, physicians had a higher level of *conscientiousness* than did the general population (Stienen et al. 2018). They also scored higher on *agreeableness* and *extraversion*. They scored lower on *neuroticism*. In the genetic research cited earlier, in which neuroticism was found to have a genetic component, physicians would seem to have less genetic weighting on this factor than the general population. Physicians did not differ from the general population on *openness to experience.*

This study indicates that physicians do, indeed, have a personality profile that is unique and differs from the general population. Because medical students also scored high in *conscientiousness* and *extraversion*, it is clear that these characteristics are stable over time. The work of the physician requires being organized, thorough, and efficient. In today's world of medical finances, efficiency commands an even higher premium, with physicians being pushed to see more patients per day than ever. In addition, physicians need to be assertive, energetic, and able to move quickly from one patient to the next—all components of *extraversion*.

Physicians scoring lower on *neuroticism* than the general population suggests that physicians are less anxious and more stable than the average person. The need to adapt to the high-stress, rapidly changing environments of residency and medical practice calls for a higher degree of emotional stability than is the case in many other professions.

The factor of *agreeableness* as a differentiator suggests that physicians are more compassionate and altruistic than the general population. Given that the work of physicians is in healing, this is not an unusual finding. This finding is likely a combination of a predisposition in people attracted to the healing arts along with reinforcement of this trait during medical training.

Cognition: Some People Are Cleverer than Others

This statement has great face validity and is the source of any number of anecdotal observations and even humor. But it is not so simple. Like many aspects in human behavior and cognition, intelligence is a complex rather than a unitary trait. Intelligence includes *how* a person thinks and not simply the totality of his or her abilities. Problem-solving, thinking conceptually, ability to reason, and the ability to analyze are all aspects of understanding intelligence.

Most studies that have tried to understand the nature of intelligence have included the study of twins and of families with adopted children. The most consistent findings in these studies is that intelligence does have a strong genetic component. These studies suggest that about 50 percent of differences in intelligence can be attributed to genetic factors. In general, individuals with parents possessing lower intelligence will likely have lower intelligence themselves. Similarly, individuals with parents possessing higher intelligence are also likely to have higher intelligence. However, there continues to be debate over whether or not intelligence can increase over time; the degree to which environmental factors can impact intelligence (education; parents reading to their children; children being exposed to certain occupations, nutrition, and even breast feeding). It is clear that environmental *and* genetic factors play a role in determining intelligence (Deary 2013).

In the general population, we would expect to have a bell curve distribution with both cognitive and interpersonal attributes. Intellectual capabilities are best understood through the use of intellectual measures such as the Wechsler Adult Intelligence Scale (WAIS). In hundreds of thousands of studies, researchers have determined that the average intelligence quotient of the population is 100 with a standard deviation of 15 (see Figure 3.3). When considering the bell curve, this means that 50 percent of the population is above 100 and 50 percent below 100.

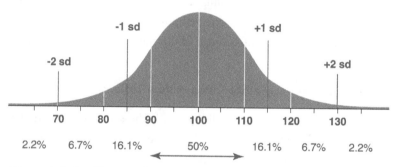

Figure 3.3 Intelligence distribution

We know that intelligence is highly genetic and likely further developed in childhood. We have postulated that the medical school admissions process selects for intelligence among other factors. What we know about physicians' intelligence comes from the most exhaustive study conducted at the University of Wisconsin (Hauser 2002). In their study of intelligence and occupational choice, physicians ranked at the very top of professions with regard to intelligence with an average IQ of about 120 (with a range of 105 to 132). Clearly, this is in some measure related to the degree of educational attainment. It is likely that those in other professions requiring the same amount of education as for physicians would score similarly. The study also concludes that occupational selection and success do not depend solely on intelligence. A myriad of social and psychosocial variables also contributes to success as a physician. However, on the basis of intelligence alone, these conclusions continue to narrow our funnel, differentiating physicians further from the general population.

Personality and Medical Specialty

Now that we have a general personality profile for physicians, we ask, are all physicians alike? Well, no, they are not. We have determined that physicians have aspects of their personalities that are different from those of the general public. Furthermore, we know that there are a myriad of specialties that physicians pursue through residencies and fellowships. Does this selection have anything to do with personality differences, or is it just random?

While there are numerous specialties in medicine (over 100), we will look at them from the standpoint of those specialties that are primarily cognitive and those that are primarily procedural. This distinction includes cognitive domain specialties such as internal medicine, pediatrics, and psychiatry. In the procedural domain, we consider specialties such as surgical specialties.

Research has been undertaken to determine whether there is a Distinct Surgical Personality (DSP). In this research, the conclusions were that surgeons rank higher in conscientiousness than do other specialties but *lower* in agreeableness. This suggests that surgeons are highly self-disciplined and prudent along with possessing a heightened sense of responsibility. However, compared with other specialties, surgeons have a lower regard for the interpersonal context (low agreeableness). This could be related to the long-held thought that the surgical theater is not a place for high emotion, but rather a place for concentration and execution (Turska 2016).

A similar study compared surgeons with the general population and determined that surgeons are lower in neuroticism, lower in extraversion, and lower in openness to experience than internists. This would seem to confirm that surgeons are more stable, able to maintain calm in the midst of crises, highly focused, and more insightful than the general population (McGreevy 2002). Again, this would seem to "fit" with the work of the surgeon. When performing one surgery after another, the role of experimenting, being highly gregarious, or becoming anxious could create challenges for surgeons. In other words, the research confirms what makes sense in the surgical theater, namely, being focused and free of distraction is critical to having the best outcomes.

In both a review of the literature, and in a comprehensive study, the authors found significant differences on some of the Big Five Personality Factors and different specialties (Figure 3.4). We have separated them into cognitive and procedural specialties (Borges and Savickas 2002; Mullola et al. 2018).

Big Five personality factors	Cognitive			Procedural		
	Pediatrics	FP/IM	Psychiatry	ObGyn	Anesthesiology	Surgery
Openness	0	0	+	−	+	−
Conscientious	−	+	−	+	−	+
Extravert	+	−	0	0	+	−
Neuroticism	+	0	−	0	−	−
Agreeable	+	+	+	−	−	−

Figure 3.4 Big five factors across specialties

Source: Borges and Savickas (2002) and Mullola et al. (2018).

Note: + indicates more than; − indicates less than; 0 indicates no difference.

The Psychology of the Physician: Integrating Research

The interaction between genotype, phenotype, and the environment all contributes to the development of personality. Using the Big Five Personality Factors and genetic research as the context for understanding the physician personality, we have been able to come to these conclusions:

1. As an occupation, physicians have higher intellectual capabilities than the general population (average IQ of 120 with a range of 105 to 132).
2. When compared with the general population, there does appear to be a *physician personality*. Physicians, as a group, score higher than the general population on:
   • conscientiousness
   • agreeableness
   • extraversion
3. Physicians as a group scored lower on neuroticism.
4. There was no difference between the general population and physicians on openness to experience.

When comparing physicians with each other (Figure 3.4), some additional differences surface.

- Procedural Physicians: As a group, physicians in this broad area are less agreeable, less neurotic and tend to be more conscientious than their cognitive counterparts. Surgeons are higher in conscientiousness than other specialties, but lower in agreeableness and neuroticism.
- Cognitive Physicians: As a group, physicians in this area are more agreeable than procedural physicians.

Five-Factor Model and the Personality of the Leader

It is folly to try and discuss the personality of the physician-leader without understanding the overall personality of leaders. Only by understanding the characteristics of effective leaders does contemplating the physician-leader personality make any sense. Fortunately, there has been significant research identifying which of the Big Five Personality Factors are beneficial for effective leadership.

In the largest study to date, a 2002 meta-analysis was conducted on over 75 previously published research projects that studied the relationship between personality and leadership. The researchers conducted both a qualitative and quantitative analysis of previously published studies that had evaluated the Big Five Personality Factors and leadership. The authors concluded, first, that the results provided support for the five-factor model in leadership research. This meta-analysis further determined that both *extraversion* and *conscientiousness* were significantly correlated with leadership effectiveness. *Extraversion* emerged as the most consistent correlate of leadership, suggesting that "both sociable and dominant people are more likely to assert themselves in group situations." *Conscientiousness* also was strongly related to leadership emergence. This is not surprising since being reliable, disciplined, and achievement-seeking are, on the surface, positive traits to have for leadership.

Agreeableness was not found to be significantly related to leadership effectiveness. Presumably, leaders that are too agreeable may be passive, overly compliant, too eager to be liked, and unwilling to "rock the boat."

Any characteristics, used in excess, can be counter-productive in leadership roles (Judge et al. 2002). As with other research, they found a *negative* correlation between *neuroticism* and effective leadership. The emotional lability, insecurity, and uncertainty of individuals scoring high in *neuroticism* work against them in leadership positions. A subsequent study even found *neuroticism* to have a negative effect on the employees' perception of ethical leadership (Gonul 2016).

In a 2018 study of leaders in various corporations, the researchers again found a significant correlation between leadership and *conscientiousness* and a significant inverse correlation between leadership and *neuroticism*. In addition, the researchers found a weak inverse relationship between *agreeableness* and authentic leadership. The authors concluded that "conscientious leaders with low level of neuroticism, who practice authentic leadership, will bring about positive social change by reducing unethical practices, improving communication with employers, employees, and consumers, and improving employee morale" (Baptiste 2018).

In an interesting expansion of work on leadership, another study looked at leadership styles and the personality traits of employees being led. Looking at both autocratic and participative leadership styles, the researchers found a significant correlation between *extraversion* in employees and their preference for a participative leader. They suggest that extraverted employees are more social and collaborative, attracting them to a participative leadership style that involves working together to make decisions with the leader (Bertsch 2017). This finding is particularly relevant to those who lead physicians, as we have already surmised that extroversion is a common personality trait among physicians.

Taken together, the research is compelling in regard to the positive role of *extraversion* and *conscientiousness* in leadership. The research also suggests a *negative* correlation between *neuroticism* and leadership. However, these correlations merely identify broad personality traits that are conducive to leading others. At an individual level, these correlations can help leaders understand which productive leadership behaviors come more naturally to them. At the same time, they must also realize that too much of a good thing can work against you. For example, the type of extraversion that displays excessive gregariousness and dominance can actually interfere with the duties of leading. Similarly, the conscientious leader that pays excessive attention to detail can actually slow work down. Agreeableness is generally well regarded in society, yet being overly *agreeable* can also interfere with being an effective leader. Overly deferential behavior, wanting to please, and avoiding difficult conversations reduce a leader's effectiveness. Our next section looks at the five-factor model as it relates to physicians in leadership roles.

The Psychology of Physicians: Implications for the Physician-Leader?

Now that we have examined the personality of the leader as demonstrated by research, we can begin to understand the traits that physician-leaders need to be most effective. We have been able to make some generalizations about the personality of physicians through the synthesis of available research and our own personal experiences in the field. We have further refined those characterizations to the individual specialty level in some cases. The intent of this chapter is not to suggest that all physicians fit into this profile. Rather, the purpose of this chapter is to describe personality traits that are common to the physician subgroup of the general population.

As a result, it is very possible that physicians making the transition to physician-leadership will do so in the context of these common physician personality traits. In general, physicians commonly possess many personality traits that would predispose them to leadership. Importantly, physician-leaders should consider how this general psychological background both contributes to and creates challenges for their success as a leader. Low *neuroticism* and high emotional stability can help physician-leaders weather the volatility and stress of leadership roles but can also inhibit vulnerability. Lack of vulnerability can make leaders less relatable and seemingly aloof to those they are attempting to lead. High levels of *conscientiousness* in leaders facilitates organization and task achievement but can also predispose leaders to be risk averse and myopic in their perspective. The energy and gregariousness of *extraversion* can help leaders be both productive and engaging. Yet the assertiveness of extraversion can bring a dominant edge to leadership that hinders open communication and collaboration. Agreeableness can foster cooperation and teamwork.

At the same time, agreeableness can cause paralysis in decision making when a consensus cannot be reached. Each personality trait brings strengths and weaknesses when it comes to leadership. Understanding the typical personality profile of a physician can help transitioning physician-leaders predict and prepare for challenges they may face while focusing their development on the areas most likely to have the greatest impact on their success as a leader.

Understanding the general personality profile of a physician is clearly beneficial. Narrowing this personality profile down to the individual medical specialty can provide even greater specificity and benefit. Using these personality profiles, physician-leaders can better understand their own predispositions, strengths, and weaknesses. Additionally, these profiles can help physician-leaders better understand the predispositions of the physicians they are tasked with leading in order to create targeted approaches and strategies.

Appropriate use of these generalizations around physician personality traits is only half the battle. Truly successful physician-leaders will need to assess where they fall as individuals within these general profiles. While physicians as a group can be aptly described with a general profile, each individual physician may or may not fit the general profile. Every physician-leader needs to understand their individual personality profile in order to best develop their leadership skills.

Coach's Corner

Psychology is a powerful tool for leaders. Possessing general knowledge about the psychological similarities within a group such as physicians is predictive and advantageous. Understanding your own psychological drivers and the distinct psychological drivers of others is a game changer.

1. **Take a personality profile test**
   - Physician-leaders must understand their own predispositions to be truly successful. Use of a reliable personality profile test can provide valuable information. We recommend assessments based on the Big Five Personality Factors. We recommend the Hogan suite of assessments and coaches (Hogan n.d.).[19]

2. **Understand yourself**

  - Using the results of your personality profile test, create a personal understanding of your Big Five Personality Factors. Personal introspection is useful, but discussion with a coach or someone who knows you well can help in this pursuit.

3. **Create a plan**

  - Once you are confident that you understand your individual personality traits, consider how each of these traits will facilitate or inhibit your success as a leader. Again, consultation with a coach can be helpful, but we will also discuss how personality traits relate to key leadership skills and behaviors in later chapters.

References

Baptiste, B. 2018. "The Relationship between the Big Five Personality Traits and Authentic Leadership." *Walden University Scholar Works.* https://scholarworks.waldenu.edu/cgi/viewcontent.cgi?article=5993 &context=dissertations (accessed May 6, 2019).

Bertsch, A., H.T.H. Nguyen, A. Alford, W. Baran, J. Reynen, M. Saeed, and J. Ondracek. 2017. "Exploring the Relationship between Personality and Preferred Leadership." *Journal of Leadership, Accountability and Ethics* 14, no. 1. http://www.na-businesspress.com/JLAE/BertschA_ Web14_1_.pdf (accessed May 6, 2019)

Borges, J., and M. Savickas. August, 2002. "Personality and Medical Specialty Choice: A Literature Review and Integration." *Journal of Career Assessment* 10, no. 3, pp. 362–80.

Costa, P.T., and R.R. McCrae. 1992. *The NEO Personality Inventory Manual.* Odessa, FL: Psychological Assessment Resources.

Deary, I.J. August, 2013. "Intelligence." *Current Biology* 23, no. 16, pp. R673–R676. https://www.sciencedirect.com/science/article/pii/ S0960982213008440 (accessed October 29, 2018).

Digman, J.M. 1990. "Personality Structure: Emergence of the Five-Factor Model." *Annual Review of Psychology* 41, pp. 417–40. doi:10.1145/ annurev.ps.41.020190.002221 (accessed October 28, 2018).

Ferguson, E., A. Sanders, F. O'Hehir, and D. James. December, 2010. "Predictive Validity of Personal Statements and the Role of the Five-Factor Model of Personality in Relation to Medical Training." *Journal of Occupational and Organizational Psychology.* https://doi .org/10.1348/096317900167056 (accessed October 29, 2018).

Gonul, K. 2016. "The Role of Personality in Leadership: Five Factor Personality Traits and Ethical Leadership." *Procedia—Social and Behavioral Sciences* 235, pp. 235–42. https://reader.elsevier.com/reader/sd/pii/S18 77042816315531?token=A2F0136D672CB51AA8383AC8C17851 97D4F2AFFB82A85EF0743E4F22EE5509301653B627DEC368B8 DC7DFBED1C4FCDCC (accessed May 6, 2019).

Hauser, R.M. August, 2002. "Meritocracy, Cognitive Ability, and the Sources of Occupational Success." Department of Sociology, Center for Demography and Ecology, The University of Wisconsin-Madison.

https://www.ssc.wisc.edu/cde/cdewp/98-07.pdf (accessed October 23, 2018).

Hogan, R. n.d. https://www.hoganassessments.com (accessed October 23, 2018).

Hogan, R., and J. Hogan. 2007. *Hogan Personality Inventory Manual.* Tulsa, OK: Hogan Assessment Systems.

Judge, T.A., J.E. Bono, R. Ilies, and M.W. Gerhardt. August, 2002. "Personality and Leadership: A Qualitative and Quantitative Review." Journal of Applied Psychology 87, no. 4, pp. 765–80. https://www.ncbi.nlm.nih.gov/pubmed/12184579 (accessed May 6, 2019).

Lievens, F., D.S. Ones, and S. Dilchert. November, 2009. "Personality Scale Validities Increase throughout Medical School." *Journal of Applied Psychology* 94, no. 6, pp. 1514–35. https://www.ncbi.nlm.nih.gov/pubmed/19916659 (accessed October 28, 2018).

McGreevy, J., and D. Wiebe. August, 2002. "A Preliminary Measurement of the Surgical Personality." *The American Journal of Surgery* 184, no. 2, pp. 121–25.

Mullola, S., C. Hakulinen, J. Presseau, D. Gimeno Ruiz de Porras, M. Jokela, T. Hintsa, and M. Elovainio. March, 2018. "Personality Traits and Career Choices among Physicians in Finland: Employment Sector, Clinical Patient Contact, Specialty and Change of Specialty." *BMC Medical Education* 18, no. 1, p. 52. https://link.springer.com/article/10.1186/s12909-018-1155-9 (accessed October 31, 2018).

Power, R., and M. Pluess. 2015. "Heritability Estimates of the Big Five Personality Traits Based on Common Genetic Variants." *Translational Psychiatry* 5, p. e604. https://doi.org/10.1038/tp.2015.96 (accessed October 31, 2018).

Stienen, M.N., F. Scholtes, R. Samuel, A. Weil, A. Weyerbrock, and W. Surbeck. 2018. "Different but Similar: Personality Traits of Surgeons and Internists—Results of a Cross-Sectional Observational Study." *BMJ Open* 8, p. e021310. doi:10.1136/bmjopen-2017-021310 (accessed October 31, 2018).

Turska, D., M. Skrzypek, A. Tychmanowicz, and T. Baran. 2016. "Concept of Distinct Surgical Personality Revisited: Personality Traits and Personal Values as Surgical Specialty Choice Predictors." *European*

Journal of Medical Technologies 1, no. 10, pp. 54–59. https://pdfs
.semanticscholar.org/62c9/68eb458aa252998ae6c096b6519817c3facd
.pdf (accessed October 31, 2018).

Vedel, A. April, 2016. "Big Five Personality Group Differences across
Academic Majors: A Systematic Review." *Personality and Individual
Differences* 92, pp. 1–10. https://www.sciencedirect.com/science/
article/pii/S0191886915300921 (accessed October 29, 2018).

CHAPTER 4

Influence: The Bedrock of Leadership

In July of 2016, the CEO of Southern Coos Hospital in Brandon, Oregon, was terminated, prior to the completion of the 18-month extension that he had been awarded. The board cited concerns that the staff had regarding the CEO's leadership style (Gooch 2016).

In January of 2017, the Summa Health CEO resigned after receiving a no-confidence vote by 240 physicians. Cited among the grievances was that he was making significant changes to the health system without consulting physicians about the impact those changes would have on patient care. As a leader, his lack of engagement with those for whom he was responsible ultimately led to his downfall (Garrett 2017).

In June of 2017, the community of Martha's Vineyard was rocked by the news that the CEO of their local hospital had been terminated after only 13 months on the job. Among the reasons for his termination were concerns about his ability to listen to and collaborate with the board, a resultant loss of confidence in him by board members, and questions about who was making the ultimate decisions (Wells 2018).

In October of 2017, the Air Force terminated the medical squadron commander of the 62nd Medical Squadron at Lewis-McChord base in Washington state. He was terminated for concerns about his fairness, favoritism, poor morale in his squadron, and his tendency to promote his religion in ways that made his airmen feel uncomfortable (Losey 2017).

In March of 2018, Brookline Trauma Center terminated their physician-founder of 35 years for accusations of employee mistreatment and creating a hostile work environment. He was accused of bullying and making employees feel denigrated and uncomfortable (The Lowell Sun 2018).

In all of the foregoing cases, the terminated health care executive failed to recognize that leadership is about more than title, position, or power. In each of these cases, the leader failed to engage others effectively in decision making, demonstrated an authoritarian command-and-control management style, or pushed a personal agenda that was not in the best interest of the organization. What each of these unsuccessful executives failed to understand is that leadership is about being able to create a followership not a dictatorship. This followership is with subordinates, superiors, peers in the organization or community, and other individuals who are critical to the success of the enterprise. The capabilities of the team are far greater than those of the individual. Leadership is about influence and leveraging the skills, capabilities, and knowledge of those with whom you work. Demonstrating power and authority alone is not successful management behavior for the long term.

Leveraging human capital capabilities within an organization requires more than simply setting an agenda, providing clear roles and responsibilities, or getting everyone strategically "on the same page." In fact, although all of these tactics are important in accomplishing major organizational initiatives, if the workforce is not engaged, the business will suboptimize or even fail. Engaging a workforce is the most essential, and fundamental, role of any leader. Successful leaders *always* have engaged organizations. Having people *wanting* to work for you, and not simply *having* to work for you, is the secret sauce of effective leadership. Employee engagement is a by-product of effective leadership *influence*, not, as many would expect, either power or authority (Beard and Weiss 2017; Roth and Conchie 2008; Sinek 2009).

Engaging the workforce and using the best leadership style is not simply a contrived *program du jour* invented by human resources. There are actual financial benefits for adopting an engaging style. In one of the most exhaustive studies on employee satisfaction and business results, it was found that companies with engaged employees outperformed their peers from 2.3 to 3.8 percent per year in long-term stock results. Over the 28 years of data, these companies outperformed their peers from 89 to 184 percent cumulatively (Edmans 2016). The financial and human benefits of adopting an influential leadership style make this a no-brainer on how to lead.

Creating Organizational Success through Influence

Using *influence* to motivate and impact change is more sustainable than either power or authority. The use of power can be effective for short-term changes, but these changes are not sustainable. Using power to intimidate or get compliance will achieve both, but only for a short time. It is clear that when employees leave companies they are typically leaving their managers. Healthy and high-performing employees will abandon heavy-handed or weak managers, leaving the company with a lower performing employee base. Employees with engaged workforces have an impact on the bottom line.

Influence is a multifaceted ability. Our formula for leadership influence is CARVE (Figure 4.1):

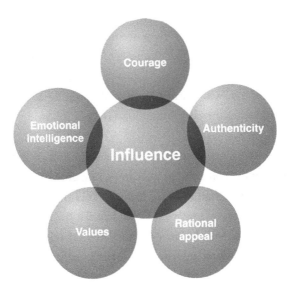

Figure 4.1 Formula for influence

Influence = Courage + Authenticity + Rational Appeal + Values + Emotional Intelligence (EQ)

Influence is a combination of deeply understanding oneself, understanding others, developing authenticity, courage, and demonstrating that the values you possess are similar to those held by the people whom you are leading. In order to become a leader with followership, and not simply compliance, mastering these skills is imperative, as we will clarify in the following section.

Leadership Characteristics of Influence: Courage

Effective leadership requires courage. Leaders must have the courage to be wrong or to fail in spite of their apprehensions and insecurities as success without risk is very limited. They must be the flag-bearers for grand ideas and goals yet open to the opinions and ideas of others. Conflict both internal and external to the organization must be embraced, for avoidance of conflict only causes problems to snowball. Too often, courage is associated with analogies about sports or war. These analogies are vivid, easy to understand, and highly limited in scope! Not only are the foxhole and football field venues limited, but the kind of courage demonstrated does not go far. These scenarios often describe courage in the face of physical danger. For the leader, the dangers are equally real. Rather than physical dangers, the leader faces potential damage to the psyche and the ego, which can be just as devastating and long lasting. Being courageous is the cornerstone of having a following and leading through influence.

In most companies, there is a covert recognition of problems that may be holding the company back or impeding growth. Often, those at the very top of the organization fail to see what is obvious to others. This lack of problem acknowledgement by leaders can be the result of a sense of hubris and ownership in having crafted the organization. It can also result from fear of embracing failure or possible challenges previously unrecognized. The failure of the senior management of Kodak to recognize the impact of digital photography is an example. Because of the personal investment in a product or direction, or because of denial, executives often fail to see the obvious. As a result, they stay the course on a path to oblivion. It is the courageous leader who is willing to publicly recognize the obvious, with the understanding that nothing can change that goes unaddressed. It is ironic that simply recognizing the unwelcome obvious can be a statement of courage. Recognizing the obvious raises a leader's credibility in any organization.

In any organization, there is a tendency toward both groupthink and agreement with those in charge. After all, they are making the big bucks, so they must know better. Being able to take a stand that is different from the group or those in charge, particularly when their idea or initiative has momentum, requires a degree of chutzpah and boldness that is out of the ordinary. This is not to say that being oppositional is a desirable trait. However, being willing to take a position that is at odds with popular opinion and being able to support the position with data is at the heart of being courageous.

One major difference between a courageous stand and one that is born of narcissism and insecurity is that a courageous leader is willing to attack a problem and not attack those who may hold a view that is different. Courageous individuals create a safe environment for others to openly disagree about an issue and not suffer consequences. Being able to brainstorm and have spirited debate is at the heart of identifying solutions and pathways that are of a higher level than routinely following the status quo.

Leadership Characteristics of Influence: Authenticity

In recent years, numerous studies have surfaced on the importance of authentic leadership. Authentic leaders behave in a genuine, sincere manner that is consistent with who they really are. Authentic leaders inspire trust and loyalty among those with whom they work. Research on authentic leadership has determined that it is a strong predictor of employee job satisfaction, organizational commitment, and work happiness (Jensen 2006). Ultimately, authentic leadership is found in three primary characteristics: congruence, humility, and vulnerability.

Congruence has two behaviors that define it. First, it is the requirement that leaders be transparent with their thoughts and feelings and that these match their behaviors. In order for leaders to be considered authentic, they must consistently ensure alignment between what they are actually thinking and feeling and the expression of those thoughts and feelings. This alignment happens both at the workplace and away from it. Congruent leaders are not different in different environments. They are consistently truth tellers who do not present a façade. This alignment requires that leaders have enough self-confidence that their behaviors are not determined by wanting to please or be liked by others. Instead, their behaviors are spontaneously and honestly a response to any situation. The best leaders will always consider their audience and use appropriate tact and diplomacy in delivering their messages without "spinning" them for political correctness or gain. Congruence is developed over time and requires consistency and the ability to be transparent.

Humility is the second quality of authenticity. Humility is the opposite of hubris. It is feeling confident enough *not* to need to be self-promoting. Humility is the recognition that, although a leader may know most of the answers to any particular subject, no one knows all of the right answers all of the time. Humble leaders recognize that the capabilities and experiences of others can contribute insights and value that they may not have. Humble leaders are open to feedback, open to seriously considering the points of views of others, willing to admit to their shortcomings and to change in the face of new and contradictory information. These leaders are as comfortable making assertions about what they know as they are in admitting when they do not know. They are willing to either share the credit or stand in the shadows altogether. Getting a job done well is more important to the humble leader than the question of who gets the credit. It is the arrogant leaders who believe there is nothing unknown to them and that their views and opinions are of a higher value than those with whom they work. Jim Collins, in his book *Good to Great,* identified humility as one of the two characteristics leaders of great companies had (the other being fierce resolve). In his study of over 1400 companies, he identified 11 that by his criteria were great. Of the CEOs of these companies, he said that "these good to great leaders never wanted to become larger-than-life heroes. They never aspired to be put on a pedestal or become unreachable icons. They were seemingly ordinary people quietly producing extraordinary results" (Collins 2001). Wow!

Vulnerability, like humility, requires a degree of comfort with oneself that allows others to "look under the hood" regarding their foibles, insecurities, and flaws. According to author and researcher Brene Brown, vulnerability is a combination of uncertainty, risk, and emotional exposure (Brown 2012). Vulnerable leaders have a willingness to risk being honest and open about who they are, in spite of judgment or disapproval.

Commonly, in competitive work environments there is subtle, but relentless, pressure for leaders to present themselves as "altogether" and without flaws. The truth is we are all flawed. Although everyone knows privately his or her own weaknesses and shortcomings, in public there is pressure to conform to the prevailing cultural expectations of being smart, assertive, capable in all situations, and knowing most, if not all, of the answers. Interestingly, it is the vulnerable leaders that are willing to acknowledge their apprehensions, lack of knowledge, or occasional foibles who have the highest level of respect and trust from their peers and subordinates. The defensive, closed off leader can be intimidating and can get conformity but will not gain a followership of healthy colleagues.

Leadership Characteristics of Influence: Rational Appeal

We always recommend that attempts to influence begin with an appeal to the rational side of those you are hoping to influence. This means beginning with intellectual reason. By initiating presentations and discussions with logic, the leader presents data and the rationale for changes that are being suggested. This concept is especially important for the physician-leader who is often responsible for influencing other physicians and members of the health care team. A phrase commonly heard in the health care setting is "In God we trust, all others bring data." The rationale must first demonstrate that the proposed change is in the best interest of the patients. Additionally, there should be benefits for the organization, its employees, and the sustaining interests of other stakeholders. If lucid and compelling arguments, grounded in logic and data, cannot be made, there is probably not a good reason to proceed. Always keep in mind that leaders shoulder the heavy responsibility for leading organizations in a manner that benefits multiple constituents. It is a courageous and daunting role!

An example of a rational appeal is that of Satya Nadella's 2014 reorganization of Microsoft. Microsoft's culture had become overly competitive, and innovation was diminishing. By sharing with the employees a common goal to reinvent business processes, build the intelligent cloud platform, and create more personal computing, Nadella was able to restructure the organization for the future. Nadella's restructuring gave employees a new sense that their work had real meaning. It was a bold plan substantiated by equally strong rationale (Troyani 2017).

One challenge relatively unique to the physician-leader centers around evidence-based medicine. In modern health care, evidence-based medicine is the gold standard. There is great confidence in having a double-blind, randomized control study with clear results to support your health care practices. Unfortunately, there is only evidence-based medicine to support about 20 percent of modern health care practice, and most of that evidence is much less powerful than a randomized control trial. To top it off, in many areas of interest, the studies are conflicting in their results, which only further muddies the waters. "Treacherous" best describes these waters for the physician-leader. They must be sure to use evidence-based medicine when the evidence is strong. At the same time, the physician-leader must recognize when the evidence is weak or unsupportive, and an initiative should not be pursued. The most challenging scenario is one that may be the most prevalent. When there is limited evidence or only early acceptance of the evidence, the physician-leader must look beyond the clinical data to determine the value of the initiative. They must take a comprehensive approach that considers both clinical and nonclinical perspectives to craft the best possible rational appeal. Once an initiative is implemented, they must follow the local results and adjust course if indicated. This is one example of where the aforementioned courage comes in handy.

While rational appeal is a tangible and correct place to start the tactical process of influence around any particular initiative or subject, emotional appeal can be equally or more compelling than rational appeal. One thing that differentiates doing work from having a career is the degree to which a person's efforts relate to the *meaning* in their lives. This is the emotional side of influence. People want to be a part of a winning team, and they want to be challenged to accomplish great things. They also want to follow a leader they trust and admire. When presented with a goal that connects them to the interests and values of the individual, both productivity and pride increase. The sock company Bombas has the goal of creating a great sock. By itself, that goal does not tug at your heartstrings. However, Bombas has the additional goal of giving one pair of socks to homeless shelters for every pair sold (noting that socks are the number one request from homeless shelters). Now, that is a goal that appeals to the *emotions* of their workers! As of this writing, they have donated 10 million pairs of socks to homeless shelters. This goal connects the work of their employees to an altruistic and transformational goal. Emotional appeal is multifaceted, but two crucial components of emotional appeal relate to the two leadership characteristics that we discuss next: values and emotional intelligence.

Leadership Characteristics of Influence: Values

One of the most important requirements for effective influencing is the alignment of the values of the leaders and those of whom they are leading. When there is great disparity between the values of the leader and those of his or her constituents, a hurdle arises that they must overcome before they can begin to listen to the leader. In fact, sharing common values with the leader contributes substantially to team members' trust in a leader (Gillespie and Matt 2004).

Followership requires that followers believe the leader is leading in their best interest as well as the company's. This comes from the leader knowing those who are being led, demonstrating a degree of empathy and commitment to them, and setting an example they would like to follow. In this era, where there are huge differences between executive compensation and the compensation of those "keeping the lights on," it is even more crucial for leaders to demonstrate that the values they have are similar to the values of those they are leading. While all promotions into greater leadership positions carry some risk, those leaders who are promoted from inside the organization have a greater chance of success than the ones appointed from the outside. Leaders from the inside are assumed to be made of the same cloth as those with whom they work unless they prove otherwise.

Shared values can exist between a leader and their employees as well as between an organization and its employees. At the organizational level, its values and its proverbial "brand" are one and the same. If the organization's brand resonates with its employees, this creates powerful influence. Ultimately, if an organization's staff shares common values with both their leaders and their organization, that is the foundation of a strong culture that will sow the seeds of influence for the leaders within. Creating this sense of common values requires communication from leadership and consistency of actions with words. However, it also requires recruiting and hiring employees who are predisposed to share the organization's values.

Leadership Characteristics of Influence: Emotional Intelligence

There is a very close relationship between leadership influence and leadership emotional intelligence, or EQ. Emotional intelligence is defined by the degree to which leaders are aware of, and manage, their emotions and the emotions of their fellow employees. Leaders with a high EQ are those who are aware of their own feelings, motivations, and behaviors as well as those of others. They are not only aware of them, but also know how to manage them for optimal results (Figure 4.2). Once again, a very robust

	Self	**Other**
Recognition	Emotional Awareness Accurate self-assessment Self-confidence	Empathy Service orientation Developing others Leveraging diversity Organizational awareness
Regulation	Self-control Trustworthiness Conscientiousness Adaptability Achievement drive Initiative	Communication Leadership Conflict management Building bonds Teamwork Collaboration

Figure 4.2 A paradigm for emotional intelligence
Source: Goleman (2001).

relationship between business results and high EQ has been documented in a meta-analysis of 19 studies (Cherniss 2013).

Not surprisingly, the first condition necessary for leaders to adopt influence as a default leadership style is to have a good understanding of what motivates them. This insight begins with the recognition that all people are flawed, and yet, all people are also exquisitely unique and possess distinct strengths. The acknowledgment of both opposing poles is equally important as together, they form the basis of one's emotions, and the ability to be intentional about behavior requires a recognition of the underlying emotions in any situation. It is the appropriate management of these emotions that becomes evident in successful leadership behavior.

The great Swiss psychiatrist, Carl Jung, discussed any unawareness we may have as being our *shadow side*. When we have insecurities and feel anxious in various situations, it is imperative to take ownership of them personally and, as appropriate, publicly. Jung noted that the failure to recognize our shadow side makes us vulnerable to unconsciously "acting out" from it. In other words, when we feel insecure but are either unaware of it or repress it, we are likely to overreact to situations in a fight-or-flight scenario. This is also true when we are unaware, or in denial, about the strengths we have. We will likely underutilize our strengths and be plagued with unnecessarily low self-esteem, not recognizing the uniqueness we can bring to any situation and lacking the courage to assert ourselves.

The second part of the EQ equation is understanding and managing the feelings of others. This can be trickier and not only involves a desire to comprehend individual uniqueness but also requires the intentionality to recognize the emotional behaviors of others and act on their behalf. Having empathy and understanding how others are motivated can result in productivity, followership, and engagement. Even more difficult is understanding the psychological foundations of others and how that manifests in the form of day-to-day behavior. That is ultimately the challenge for all leaders as this understanding is necessary for them to succeed in their duty to provide emotional and psychological support to their employees. True success in this regard provides an incredible source of emotional appeal and influence for the leader.

Case Study

Being Right or Being Successful?

A small, growing hospital called us about assisting in the onboarding of a new chief medical officer (CMO) whom they had just promoted. Their prior CMO had recently retired, and the CEO was intent on promoting from within. As the CEO reviewed internal candidates for the position, she decided to take a chance on a young, up and coming physician who was a very good surgeon but had little management experience. The surgeon had been very successful in the surgery theater, where he was known as someone who was very insightful, confident, and skillful. In addition, he had the reputation of being direct, authoritative, and tolerating no nonsense. The CEO believed that these were the very skills needed in the CMO position, in which the retiring CMO, who lacked them, had been less than effective.

Shortly after being promoted into the CMO position, the CEO began hearing complaints from other physicians about the heavy-handed nature of the new, energetic CMO whom she had promoted. The concerns were all of a similar nature: the CMO was being authoritarian, not listening well to the ideas of others, abrasive in delivery, very certain in his point of view. When the CEO confronted the new CMO with these concerns, the CMO initially got defensive, noting that the CEO had said she wanted changes to be made. The CEO countered that it was not the *what* of his approach but the *how*. With this realization, they both agreed that, in order for the new CMO to be effective, some leadership coaching could be of great help. At that point, we were engaged to assist.

In our initial interview with the CMO, we discussed what had made him successful as a surgeon. In the surgery theater, he had been the central authority in the room. He was the leader, the authority, and the choreographer. In that role, he had to make quick decisions, be very directive, and leave little room for discussion or ambiguity. He was a machine! He wrongly believed that by having the title of CMO with the commensurate authority, people would respond much as they had in the operating room. He was perplexed that when applying the same behaviors that had made him successful in surgery to his new role, he was not getting the same results. However, he could see clearly that he had to make some changes in order to be successful in the CMO position.

Over time and through a process of coaching and administering a 360-degree assessment, we helped him understand that the kind of behaviors necessary for exercising leadership were quite different from those for being a top-notch surgeon. His high *conscientiousness* (and perfectionism) with his low *agreeableness* worked well in the operating room but not as well in managing his team. Being an effective leader requires listening to those whom you manage and support. Collaboration, negotiation, interpersonal sensitivity, dialogue, and, most importantly, patience are essential behaviors for becoming an effective leader. Except for patience and dialogue in some circumstances, these behaviors would have all interfered with performing successful surgery. Because he was motivated to succeed and willing to listen and change his behavior, he became a very effective CMO. The transition was not without some pain, repairing relationships, and "eating some crow," but the CMO was ultimately able to make the transition from being a very successful surgeon to being a successful physician-leader.

Influence and the Implications for the Physician-Leader

Creating influence is the essence of leadership for any leader. The power derived from title and authority is at best marginally effective and can only be used sparingly. Long-term, sustained, and successful leadership is born only out of the amorphous skill we call influence. Although this chapter addresses influence primarily with regard to a leader's employees, influence is also of paramount importance with peers and even superiors. The tactics of influence hold true regardless of the subject group. Few other types of leader rely on influence as much as the physician-leader. Often caught between the worlds of the clinician and the administrator, the physician-leader frequently carries little to no authority in either realm. To their physician colleagues, these leaders will always be peers to a large extent. To their administrative colleagues, these leaders are often viewed, at least partially, as outsiders. To be successful, physician-leaders must master the art of influence.

There are a couple of potential challenges to creating influence that all physician-leaders should be aware of. As we discussed in Chapter 3, physicians as a profession exhibit some common psychological traits. Low neuroticism (high emotional stability) is common to many physicians.

This can be a hindrance in creating influence as it can impair authenticity and vulnerability, making the physician less relatable to others. Intentionality in the areas of congruence and vulnerability can help mitigate this for many physician-leaders. We have also discussed that agreeableness tends to vary in physicians by specialty. It is important for physician-leaders to have an accurate assessment of their agreeableness. Focus should be directed toward finding the proper balance in this area to create influence. Physician-leaders who are low in agreeableness tend to struggle with creating influence, whereas physician-leaders who are too high in agreeableness tend to struggle with using their influence. In fact, it is a common mistake among new physician-leaders to default to acting as a mediator among other physicians, describing the landscape and helping the group come to consensus. While this may not seem like the worst thing in the world, a leader is not merely a mediator. A leader, by role, is supposed to be more informed and have more ability and time to analyze any given topic. The physician-leader must be more than a mediator. They must develop and wield influence so that they can guide the group and organization to a successful outcome. Influence for them includes developing respect for their expertise and opinion so that they are true leaders and not merely facilitators.

Finally, you will recall that, contrary to the leadership arena, the clinical arena is one that is predicated on the authority of the physician. The clinical physician conducts their job using orders, and they are the ultimate clinical authority. Creating influence is a paradigm shift for many physicians moving into leadership roles for precisely this reason. Awareness of this fact and attention to the tactics discussed in this chapter can help them overcome this barrier.

Coach's Corner

Influence is the primary virtue and engine of leadership, not authority. Rank and title do not confer lasting leverage. There are many aspects that contribute to creating influence and followership. The successful leader will develop and employ the foundational skills detailed in this chapter to create influence, manage change, and drive results in their organizations.

1. **Give up on the concept of authority**
   - Consider when and how authority can be used to lead. Identify the present and future challenges created by using authority to accomplish change. Continue this exercise until you are convinced that leading through only authority is unsustainable at best and ineffective at worst.

2. **Determine your ideal leadership style**
   - Using the CARVE model presented in this chapter, reflect on the strengths and opportunities in your personal leadership style. The best leaders develop their own unique style that encompasses foundational leadership skills while embracing their own personality.

3. **Be patient**
   - Very few great leaders are born that way, and creating influence takes time. Consider this endeavor the core work of leadership. Give it your constant effort and attention, but be patient. The progress can be imperceptible at times, but the end result is monumental.

References

Beard, M., and A. Weiss. 2017. *The DNA of Leadership: Creating Healthy Leaders and Vibrant Organizations.* New York, NY: Business Expert Press.

Brown, B. 2012. *Daring Greatly: How the Courage to Be Vulnerable Transforms the Way We Live, Love, Parent and Lead.* New York, NY: Avery.

Cherniss, C. April, 2013. "The Business Case for Emotional Intelligence." *Consortium for Research on Emotional Intelligence in Organizations. Yale University.* http://www.eiconsortium.org/reports/business_case_ for_ei.html (accessed November 19, 2018).

Collins, J. 2001. *Good to Great.* New York, NY: Harper Collins Publishers.

Edmans, A. March, 2016. "28 Years of Stock Market Data Shows a Link between Employee Satisfaction and Long-Term Value." *Harvard Business Review, Organizational Culture.* https://hbr.org/2016/03/28-years-of-stock-market-data-shows-a-link-between-employee-satisfaction-and-long-term-value (accessed November 19, 2018).

Garrett, A. January, 2017. "Summa CEO Thomas Malone Resigns: What Happens Next at Summa Remains Unclear." *Akron Beacon Journal.* https://www.ohio.com/akron/writers/betty-linfisher/summa-ceo-thomas-malone-resigns-what-happens-next-at-summa-remains-unclear (accessed November 17, 2018).

Gillespie, N.A., and L. Matt. 2004. "Transformational Leadership and Shared Values: The Building Blocks of Trust." *Journal of Managerial Psychology* 19, no. 6, pp. 588–607. https://doi.org/10.1108/026839 40410551507 (accessed November 20, 2018).

Goleman, D. 2001. "An EI-Based Theory of Performance." In *The Emotionally Intelligent Workplace*, eds. C. Cherniss and D. Goleman. San Francisco, CA: Jossey-Bass.

Gooch, K. August, 2016. "Southern Coos Hospital CEO Terminated." *Becker's Hospital Review.* https://www.beckershospitalreview.com/hospital-executive-moves/southern-coos-hospital-ceo-terminated.html (accessed November 17, 2018).

Jensen, S.M. December, 2006. "Entrepreneurs as Authentic Leaders: Impact on Employees' Attitudes." *Leadership & Organization Development Journal* 27, no. 8, pp. 646–66. https://doi.org/10.1108/01437730610709273 (accessed November 20, 2018).

Losey, S. October, 2017. "Air Force Medical Squadron Commander Fired, under Investigation." *Air Force Times.* https://www.airforcetimes.com/news/your-air-force/2017/10/16/air-force-medical-squadron-commander-fired-under-investigation (accessed November 17, 2018).

Roth, T., and B. Conchie. 2008. *Strengths Based Leadership: Great Leaders, Teams, and Why People Follow.* New York, NY: Gallup Press.

Sinek, S. 2009. *Start with Why: How Great Leaders Inspire Everyone to Take Action.* New York, NY: Portfolio Books.

The Lowell Sun. March, 2018. "Renowned Trauma Center Fires Its Medical Director." March 8, 2018. *The Lowell Sun.* http://www.lowellsun.com/breakingnews/ci_31720242/renowned-trauma-center-fires-its-medical-director (accessed November 17, 2018).

Troyani, L. May, 2017. "3 Examples of Organizational Change Done Right." *Tiny Pulse.* https://www.tinypulse.com/blog/3-examples-of-organizational-change-and-why-they-got-it-right (accessed November 20, 2018).

Wells, J. March, 2018. "Court Documents Shine New Light on Hospital, CEO Dispute." *Vineyard Gazette.* https://vineyardgazette.com/news/2018/03/15/court-documents-shine-new-light-hospital-ceo-dispute (accessed November 17, 2018).

SECTION 2

Execution in Leadership

CHAPTER 5

Strategy and Visioning: Creating Order from Chaos

While consulting with a hospital, the chief medical officer (CMO) was lamenting the lack of success of the hospital's strategic planning process. At the chief operating officer's (COO's) urging, the senior staff conducted an offsite retreat, facilitated by the CMO, to create a 3-year strategic plan. The outcome of the retreat was the framework of a strategy focused on increasing the quality of the patient experience while continuing to grow hospital patient volumes. The senior team identified four major initiatives to accomplish the strategy and charged the CMO with getting them implemented.

The CMO subsequently met with forty skeptical leaders throughout the hospital to help each of them create goals for their areas to implement the overall strategic initiative. These leaders had been the subject of numerous previously failed organizational and management development programs that were begun but never completed. The CMO planned to follow up with each leader on a quarterly basis to both monitor their progress and assist as needed. However, as with previous similar initiatives, within 3 months the strategy had been put on the shelf, having given way to the urgencies each day brings to a hospital. The CMO, already swamped with his regular job, had difficulty following up as promised. In addition, the CMO received little support from either the CEO or the chief financial officer (CFO) to continue the process. They argued that the hospital was already successfully running in the black and receiving some important national health care awards. Was a strategic planning process really necessary or just another distraction? Needless to say, the following year's planning was primarily budgetary and only for the subsequent year. The strategy and its four major initiatives comprised yet another failure. Does this sound familiar?

The hospital leadership failed to recognize that the greatest benefit of strategic planning lies in making a good organization a great one
through the discipline of preparation, forecasting, analysis, and relentless follow-up. They fell victim to the greatest threat to strategic planning, and, ultimately, organizational improvement—entropy. Entropy
is rooted in not understanding the value of having a mission, vision,
and strategies; not having senior support; being overwhelmed by the
perceived volume of work involved; not having a complete process to
execute. It is always easier for an organization to excuse itself by addressing the urgent at the expense of the important. In health care, especially,
there is *always* the urgent!

Elements of Strategy

Organizations that are serious about growth and sustainability always prioritize establishing their mission, their vision, and core strategies. This
process is crucial for organizations, no matter what the size or industry.
They give organizations direction and momentum while serving to engage their employees. Because these concepts are so misused, and often
misaligned, we will review them here.

Mission: The mission of any organization describes its reason for ex-
istence and provides the *parameters* that define the products, services, and
markets in which the company will compete. This is crucial for any company to effectively establish itself and align its employees' behaviors with
the organizational goals. A good mission answers three questions:

- **What** does the organization do?
- **Who** are the organization's end users?
- **How** does the organization perform its tasks?

The organization's mission is as important for what it *excludes* as for
what it includes. For instance, in health care, a hospital provides medical
services (what) to patients (who) through highly qualified medical staff
(how). This mission can be narrowed further if the hospital specializes in
a particular disease process (cancer, drug and alcohol recovery), narrowing
its patient base and the kind of specialists that provide services. It is clear,

however, that the hospital is *not* in the retail or food business, although physical space may be leased to companies for whom selling within a hospital is their expertise.

Once an organization's mission is established, it changes only when there have been dramatic changes in the market, industry, or products and services. It is when organizations begin dabbling in areas outside their core mission that problems usually occur. For instance, Starbucks is known for providing high-end coffee (what) to customers willing to pay a premium (who) through baristas in their coffee shops (how). In 2010, Starbucks, aiming to increase its customer traffic later in the day by offering an "Evening" program, ventured into serving alcohol and tapas. Although it eventually had an Evening program in over 400 stores, it discontinued the program in early 2017, claiming that it had failed to attract the kind of customers it had hoped it would. Starbucks had strayed from its core mission, changing the what, who, and how of its organization (Team 2017).

Vision: The vision of any company is a statement about what the company wants to be in the future. It is aspirational in nature and provides a clear focus for the business. It should evoke the passions of those in the organization. A vision can be about growth (bigger or the biggest), quality (better or best), or contributing significantly to mankind (e.g., eradicating cancer). However, the vision is more of a compass than a roadmap to the future. It is not tied to details. It is clear, memorable, and concise. A good example of a vision statement is that of Habitat for Humanity, "a world where everyone has a decent place to live." In health care, MD Anderson's vision is "to be the premier cancer center in the world, based on the excellence of our people, our research-driven patient care, and our science. We are Making Cancer History."

Unlike the mission statement, the vision can change over time depending on changing conditions (maybe the company has achieved its goal of being the best or biggest; or, like Kodak, the need for its original services has diminished). Typically, a company's vision will be reviewed on an annual basis. However, some visions, like the one for Habitat for Humanity, are so big and broad that they would change only if the original mission of the organization changed (such as adding the goal of feeding the world as well as housing it).

Strategy: Once a mission and vision have been established, companies create a set of strategies to accomplish the vision. These strategies are small in number, and they identify the most critical initiatives that need to be accomplished to achieve the organization's mission. Strategies take the vision to deeper levels of detail and become more tactical and tangible. In order to move from the conceptual to the execution stage, each part of the business, each function, and each service line needs to develop more specific tactics that align with each strategy, assigning owners, timelines, and processes for monitoring the tasks.

Case Study

Setting a Vision: Refocusing for Better Results

A large health care system had recently appointed a new physician-leader CEO to manage its growing regional business. The new CEO had been a physician within the system who had moved up the ranks to increasingly broader leadership roles. She was well respected as a leader and well liked. She had experienced success in her previous roles, and the board of directors saw her promotion as the next logical step in her career and in the evolution of the system.

However, once she was in her role at the top of the organization, she began to panic. In previous roles, she had always had someone above her, and even peers, with whom she could confer. Now she felt strangely alone and isolated. In large measure, her anxiety was related to her recognition that the system had grown quickly with no forethought given to whether this growth was either manageable or sustainable. Instead, the organization's growth was opportunistic rather than intentional. This resulted in having a system that was unbalanced with regard to types of patients, excessive services, and a strange mix of physician specialties within the system. These problems all seemed daunting and out of control. She saw the need for the organization to develop a multiyear strategy, something that had not been employed in the prior administration. She called us for a consultation.

At our initial meeting, the CEO laid out her concerns about how unwieldy the system had become. This sent her mind racing to find ways she could make changes to address the numerous concerns she had. She had developed pages and pages of notes on ways to address the problems. Immediately, we were able to see that she had fallen victim to the tendency of seeing all of the trees but not the forest. Without stepping back to see context, she was reactively addressing one problem after the other in a tactical manner, without looking at the greater need to have a strategic plan. She was figuratively rearranging the deck chairs on the Titanic.

We helped her focus on two major issues. The first was that, in any organization, a very well-understood, articulated, and communicated strategy is the foundation for everything else that happens: structure, processes, people, programs, and so forth. Making changes in the absence of a very clear strategy perpetuates the problems, rather than resolving them. The second, and equally compelling, issue was that the essence of strategy lies in choosing what *not* to do, according to the wise counsel of Harvard professor Michael Porter. By trying to be all things to all people, you fail to be of maximum benefit to anyone! New CEOs often fall into the trap of trying to prove to their board, staff, and constituents that they can do it all. As a result, they tend to say *yes* to everything and fail to look at what is realistic out of the fear of disappointing others. With the full support of the board, the CEO asked us to facilitate a strategy-setting process to create a longer-term context for the organization.

The strategy development process lasted several weeks and required looking at the bigger external issues such as the following: What are the needs of the communities being served? What are the resources required to serve these needs? Which of these needs are already, or can be, well served by other community resources? What services can the health care system provide that are in the best interest of both the community and the health care system?

By beginning with larger questions like these, differentiating between what the health care system can do and what it *should* do became clearer. By narrowing the settings, services, and patient needs that the health care system *should* address, creating a strategy became a manageable endeavor. Once the strategy had been created, the process continued through aligning the organization to the new strategy. That meant reconsidering the organizational structure, processes, people, and services. Implementing that strategy resulted in some short-term pain, with the closure of some clinics and the reduction or elimination of some services. Within a year following the strategy development, organization realignment, and communication, the health care system had a coherent plan that was meeting the needs of their target patient group, with the highest impact services and the right number of resources to address these needs. An added bonus was that the system was beginning to see a profit!

Purpose of Strategy: Bringing Order from Chaos

The purpose of creating a strategy is twofold. First, and most obviously, a strategy provides a glimpse into the future of an organization and the direction toward which the leaders of the organization want to take it. Second, and more importantly, a good strategy creates a framework for all of the work in an organization toward a common vision. It is the link that connects, and aligns, the work of those in the organization to the mission, vision, and goals of the organization. This linkage is crucial for high levels of employee engagement, motivation, and productivity. This linkage has implications for fundamental issues like organizational culture and climate; the stability of jobs; the potential for upward mobility, compensation, and job satisfaction. The better the strategy, the clearer the linkage. The clearer the linkage, the greater the likelihood of high employee engagement.

In a broad sense, setting strategy year over year ensures that the organization is not simply working on a number of unrelated and misaligned initiatives. Strategy setting is a consistent process of initially bringing order out of chaos and, subsequently, refining the strategies needed to accomplish the organization's vision (Figure 5.1). A well-designed strategy not only gets everyone marching in the same direction but also provides momentum for accomplishing the organization's vision. In a high-functioning organization, the strategy cascades down to each function or business unit in the organization. Every function or service line within an organization should have its own strategies that are aligned with the organization's strategy and provide employees with greater specificity with regard to their work. This takes the strategy from

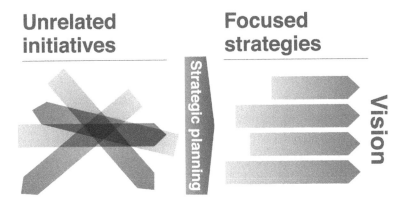

Figure 5.1 Strategic planning coordination

the more conceptual level to greater degrees of tactical and practical implementation.

Strategy Development

There are a variety of established approaches to strategic planning and thousands of consultants and facilitators available as guides. Whether an organization invests in an external resource or undertakes the challenge of strategic planning internally, the basics will remain the same.

Commitment of time and effort to properly conduct the basics of strategic planning will assist any organization in creating a vision, defining core strategies, and translating those core strategies into operational tactics. Keep in mind that strategy development is rarely effective as an individual endeavor. Success requires input from organizational leaders and stakeholders in a collaborative fashion.

Understanding the current state of the organization is a necessary component of strategic planning. A common tool that can be used is a SWOT analysis. Essentially, this is brainstorming designed to identify the organization's strengths, weaknesses, opportunities, and threats. Understanding the current state often requires a review of the organization's history and the milestones that have shaped that history. In our experience, this is often an eye-opening endeavor for those involved, and we are no longer surprised to discover that leaders do not truly understand their own organizations.

Understanding the landscape is another basic and required component of strategy development. Apart from understanding your own organization, it is essential to understand the external environment, including your customers and your competition. Who are your customers, and what are their needs? Who are your competitors, and what are their strategies? It is also important to identify external trends and drivers such as the government and legislation, societal and cultural factors, or financial markets. An organization must understand the landscape within which it exists in order to craft a successful strategy.

Identifying core strategies is an obvious step in the strategic planning process. Using the information learned about the current state of the organization and the external landscape, leaders can effectively establish a vision and core strategies for their organization. Core strategies or goals should adhere to the principles discussed in the next section. These core strategies and goals define what an organization should be focusing on and doing. Just as important, they define what the organization should not be focusing on.

Once the core strategies are identified, the organization must cascade and *execute the strategic plan.* It is incumbent on leadership to communicate the vision and core strategies throughout the organization so that each operational unit can create its action plans and tactics designed to achieve the core strategies. Identification and communication of timelines is crucial. Strategic plans should be forward thinking and long term on the scale of one year and usually multiple years. Depending on the specific organization, the exact timeline will vary, but identifying and communicating it is always required. Execution also requires identifying and tracking the metrics required for the organization to know whether it is successful in pursuing its core strategies and goals.

Updating the strategic plan is the final basic component of the process. Strategic planning is not a singular, quantized event. It is an ongoing, never-ending process. Once created, the strategic plan needs to be evaluated and updated on a regular basis, usually annually. At times, the organization will determine that enough internal or external factors have changed so that an update is not sufficient. In this case, the organization can start from scratch, fully performing every stage of the strategic planning process.

Principles of Strategy and Goal Creation

When creating any strategy, the steps are simple, but the execution can be difficult. The basis for any effective strategy is good information. The better the information, the more likely a strategy can succeed. With poor or incomplete information, creating a strategy can range from difficult to impossible. Assuming the mission and vision are clear, the question always arises about how many goals an organization should have and how detailed they should be. This is answered by two observations: The Law of Parsimony and Goals versus Accomplishment.

The *Law of Parsimony* is a psychological principle, also called the "Principle of Economy." The problem-solving theory of Occam's razor is often cited in this regard. William Occam was a thirteenth century English Franciscan monk and philosopher. He created the maxim that when looking at a number of possible hypotheses, the simplest explanation is usually the best. This is another way of encouraging people to see the obvious. In our work, we have found that the more complicated goal setting becomes, the less likely the goals will be executed. An applicable acronym could be Keep it Simple Stupid (the KISS method).

It is also important to consider the *number* of goals, strategies, or initiatives to set. The Covey organization has conducted research on the number of goals set and the likelihood of their accomplishment. Their research has found, unequivocally, that the fewer the goals a company or individual has, the more likely the goals will be accomplished. Figure 5.2 illustrates this research.

# of Goals	1–3	4–10	11–20
Goals successfully completed	1–3	1–2	0

Figure 5.2 Goals versus accomplishment

Source: McChesney, Covey, and Huling (2012).

On the face of it, setting fewer goals of higher impact makes perfect sense. You want to invest the organization's time, energy, and resources on those few initiatives that will make the most difference.

Goal Definition

In our work with organizations, we have identified the criteria for a "good goal." For a goal to be worthy of all of the work and effort that will be required to accomplish it, the goal needs to meet certain criteria. We call these criteria the HUGS method of goal development (Beard and Weiss 2017).

1. **Huge**: Any goal worth setting should be greater than what is currently being done and at least somewhat of a stretch to accomplish. Otherwise, it is only incremental and included in the normal work of employees. However, it must also be realistic. Goals that are too high or those that are too easily achieved are equally unmotivating. It is important to set goals that motivate without overwhelming. Keeping in mind the *Law of Parsimony*, goals can be big but should not be overly complex. So in this case, "huge" means ambitious and inspirational but not large in complexity.

2. **Ubiquitous**: Good goals affect the broader organization as opposed to a few departments or business units. These goals will be seen by those in the organization as synergistic with repercussions for all. The more generalizable a goal is, the more impact it will have on the organization in the long term. A ubiquitous, far-reaching goal will have positive consequences across the organization and across customers, creating a true win-win scenario.

3. **Groundbreaking**: Disruption has become the new catchword for innovation. Goals that bring about innovative solutions will help a service line or function create separation from the competition in the market. Innovation should be not simply a solution that is different from the status quo but also one that provides greater benefit for the end user. In that sense, any innovation must be linked back to customer data. Groundbreaking goals typically bring solutions to customers that include ease of use or access, less expense, higher quality, timelier delivery, or unique uses for existing products and services.

4. **Strategic:** Understanding the *context* for developing a strategic plan is a prerequisite for having a strategy that can be successful in the longer term. Being strategic means that the goals and objectives created will be in the long-term interest of the organization. To understand the culture of the organization; what the organization can, and cannot, tolerate; the appetite of the organization to change at a specified pace; and being realistic about the resources that an organization has available to use for change are all considerations that are strategic. Understanding context is a key requirement of a "good goal."

By adhering to the HUGS method in goal setting, the organization will be able to ensure that its goals are meaningful, consistent with the organization's vision, and move from the status quo to the aspirational.

The Physician-Leader: Challenges and Opportunities

Understanding the value of mission and vision along with the creation and execution of strategies and goals can be daunting for any organization. These challenges are only more pronounced in health care. All health care organizations share the common purpose of improving patient health. This common purpose is the unquestioned foundation for the mission and vision of every health care organization. As a result, efforts toward defining mission and vision can feel unnecessary and redundant. At a glance, all health care-related missions and visions can sound the same, adding no real value. The reality that many health care organizations are not adept at defining their mission and vision in a meaningful way only reinforces this perception.

Clinicians and nonclinicians alike are frequently presented with their organization's mission and vision. Inevitably, what they hear is "provide great care to patients." Why would anyone waste time and effort to simply restate the obvious? Again, the Law of Parsimony is probably the best answer to this question. Yes, all health care organizations care for patients, but truly successful organizations create a mission and vision not simply to restate the obvious but rather to refine the obvious. An effective mission and vision in a health care organization defines what that organization does and what it aspires to be primarily by defining its limits. What is it that the organization does not do? What does it not want to be?

A community hospital may want to have only a local or regional impact as opposed to a national or international one. A cancer center may aspire to diversify into other service lines, but that may or may not be a good idea. A postacute care facility is unlikely to have acute care in its mission. Academic medical centers and medical schools often refer to the triple threat of clinical care, education, and research. Perhaps some would be better served to accept that the triple threat is unachievable for them and should not be part of their mission or vision. So, although it may seem that the mission and vision of a health care organization is simple and preordained, the most successful of these organizations employ the methods discussed in this chapter to refine their path to success. As always, the devil is in the details, particularly in health care!

It is no surprise that physician-leaders have some unique challenges to consider when tackling the task of strategic planning. While their intelligence and analytical ability are major advantages in this endeavor, there are some common pitfalls that they should watch for. Clinical care is often acute care that requires clinicians to focus on the short term as opposed to the long term. Strategic planning requires leaders to think about the future, using the present only as a foundation. The "do no harm"-founded risk aversion of many physician-leaders can result in strategic plans that lack aspiration and inspiration. Finally, adhering to the Law of Parsimony requires successful prioritization. Prioritization for a leader is different from that for a clinician. A clinician prioritizes in order to determine what is more important or time sensitive and that should henceforth be done first. At the same time, the clinical setting usually requires that all the items on the list, or checklist in this case, must be done. If all the clinical tasks are not completed, the patient may have an adverse outcome. For the leader, prioritization includes not only creating a rank order for the list, but drawing a line on the list and accepting that the items below that line will simply not be done. Too many goals for a leader will result in fewer goals being achieved.

Remember that many physicians are high in conscientiousness from a psychological perspective. This conscientiousness is a strength for physicians in the clinical setting but can make it difficult to prioritize in a way that requires some items to be forsaken. Because of this psychological predisposition, many physicians transitioning into leadership roles experience discomfort with an administrative "checklist" that is infinite. They often work long hours only to go home and feel high levels of anxiety over the tasks that they were unable to complete. No doubt, physicians suffer from this in the clinical setting as well, but it is even more pronounced in the administrative setting as the coping mechanisms will differ, and a different approach to prioritization is required.

From the psychological perspective, we also learned that the factor of *extraversion* is higher in physicians than in the general population. Physicians high in extraversion are assertive, gregarious, and energetic. They are able to easily meet others in a variety of settings. This is a great characteristic for leading strategy development *in the right doses*. However, this same assertiveness that brings energy to a process can be overwhelming, or even intimidating, when used to excess. Any effective strategy development requires multiple inputs. The potential domination of the extraverted personality may discourage others from making worthy contributions of their ideas and solutions and may thus be disruptive. In addition, the strategy development process requires patience along with energy and discipline. Highly energetic leaders can create a pace that exceeds what is required for the process to be thorough and successful.

The fact that physicians are higher in *agreeableness* than the average population bodes well for working with a team to develop strategy. Agreeable individuals are cooperative and collaborative, both being desirable characteristics for the planning process. However, agreeableness carried to an extreme can lead to a desire to be liked and to please, rather than doing what is best for the institution. Once again, physician-leaders need to balance their ability to work effectively with others with a need to be overly deferential or pleasing. As cited in Chapter 3, *agreeableness* can complicate the decision-making process when people agree to something that they do not actually support just to reach a consensus without offending anyone.

As we think about the strategy development process, in light of the physician-leader's personality, it is imperative that the physician-leader regulate their strengths and recognize their weaknesses. Balance, as always, is paramount.

Coach's Corner

A thoughtful and defined mission and vision is crucial to the success of every health care organization. Paired with concise strategies and appropriate goals to create a comprehensive strategic plan, organizations can achieve alignment of efforts in their operating units and departments to accomplish the seemingly impossible!

1. **Review your organization's/department's mission, vision, strategies, and goals**
   - Does this strategic plan have enough specificity to provide direction and alignment? If not, how might you employ a strategic planning process to achieve this goal?
2. **Understand yourself**
   - Reflecting on your personality and psychology, identify the strengths and weaknesses that you bring to the strategic planning process.
3. **Find balance**
   - Develop a personal approach to the strategic planning process that balances your strengths and weaknesses.

References

Beard, M., and A. Weiss. 2017. *The DNA of Leadership: Creating Healthy Leaders and Vibrant Organizations.* New York, NY: Business Expert Press.

McChesney, C., S. Covey, and J. Huling. 2012. *The 4 Disciplines of Execution.* New York, NY: Simon & Schuster.

Team, T. January, 2017. "Starbucks Is Ending Its 'Evening' Beer and Wine Program." *Forbes.* https://www.forbes.com/sites/greatspeculations/2017/01/13/starbucks-is-ending-its-evenings-program/#128beeaf40c4 (accessed December 11, 2018).

CHAPTER 6

High-Performing Teams

Long Beach Memorial uses interdisciplinary "huddles" to address patient length of stay. Hospital medical, nursing, and administrative leadership plus a pharmacist, social worker, case manager, and rehabilitation therapist round daily to see every patient hospitalized for more than 3 days. They create three goals for each patient. As a result, the average length of stay has decreased from 5.8 days on the respiratory medical floor to 4.4 days in 1 year (Wood 2002).

Cleveland Clinic trains team members together in their simulation center to respond to emergent situations such as cardiac arrest or stroke. This practice has been a result of numerous studies demonstrating that, when health care teams train together, they can reduce morbidity and mortality. Consequently, they have been able to reduce patient mortality by having interdisciplinary teams focus on these emergent situations simultaneously and arrive at more potent solutions than any one discipline would have autonomously.

Increasingly, hospitals are using interdisciplinary health care teams to solve complex patient health issues. This evolution is a result of understanding that the interaction between patient health and health care solutions has become too complex for a single person or discipline to address. However, physician-led and patient-focused teams are only one way that hospital physicians are leading teams. As of 2014, five percent of hospital leaders are physicians, and that number is expected to increase rapidly as the broader health system moves toward value-based care (Angood 2014). Physicians are also emerging in formal leadership roles such as medical director, chief medical officer, and chief operating officer. These physician-leadership roles all have one thing in common: the need to manage a diverse team, often with both clinical and nonclinical members.

In these leadership roles, it is not just a doctor listening to a patient or another doctor. Rather, they are gathering the input of multiple disciplines to make the best decisions regarding patients, service lines, and organizations. In this regard, physicians serve as team builders, motivators, communicators, and change agents. This shift from the doctor–patient focus to focusing on larger organizational issues requires that physicians acquire, or broaden, skills for leading diverse teams. They must acquire a new set of competencies, including team-building, communication skills, business intelligence in finance, marketing, strategy formulation, information technology, and various other areas to steer the health care organizations of a complex system in flux (Angood 2014).

First and foremost, they must become effective team leaders. This requires that the physician change their customary way of thinking about health care: he or she no longer presides over a doctor–patient encounter, with everyone else in a supporting position, but is now the leader of a team who is more of a facilitator and coequal than the central figure (Weir 2018). Shifting from being primarily the authority in a doctor–patient relationship to being a choreographer, facilitator, and coordinator of a group with diverse skill sets is critical for success in these leadership roles.

Structure of the Physician-Led Team

The role of a physician on any team can vary greatly from designated team leader to team member to team consultant. It is important for physicians to realize their potential impact on a team. They are unique in that, regardless of the team or their designated role, the team will always view them as physicians. What does that mean? In the health care setting, it often means inherent respect as a subject matter expert and leader, regardless of whether or not that respect is warranted. Expertise is assumed. As such, any physician on any team in the health care setting has the opportunity to either positively impact or be disruptive to the team. This power should never be underestimated. By simply being active and engaged, the physician will be a leader of the team, whether formal or informal. In the section that follows, we address the potential roles of the physician as the designated, formal team leader.

Depending on the physician's role in the organization, the scale and scope of the team will vary. Each team has different challenges associated with it, depending on its unique purpose. What is important across *all* kinds of teams is the particular manner in which the physician-leader *frames* the issues or problems for the team. A frame is a set of assumptions that shapes how we see a situation. Health care has been typically steeped in the frame of individual expertise, provided by separate experts for solving patient problems and optimal care. This is the traditional, but *antiquated*, frame in the health care environment. In today's health care environment, interdependence of the work is critical, and individual expertise alone is no longer sufficient to produce optimal results (Fibuch and Ahmed 2018). The physician-leader will need to create a frame for teams and organizations that is broad, collaborative, recognizes the contribution of multiple and varied sources of information, and reduces the potential for silos. The physician-leader must create a psychologically safe environment where all thoughts are valued and team members freely discuss differences of opinions without repercussions. Typically, physician-led teams are of three varieties, listed here from least to most complex (Edmonson 2015):

1. **Problem-focused**: These teams are formed to address specific processes or technical challenges (e.g., patient throughput, reducing handoffs, electronic medical records (EMR) implementation). The problems are common, ever-evolving and, at times, require the team to either reconvene or reconstitute as the same issue recurs yet again. These teams have a single focus and are time limited. The team process is typically iterative and relatively simple in nature. The process consists of clearly identifying the problem and its impacts, brainstorming ideas for resolution or data collection (e.g., research or best practices), identifying best solutions, implementing, and measuring the results for process improvement. Once the problem is sufficiently resolved, the team disbands. In this role, the physician-leader acts as a facilitator/director/delegator.

   Physician-leader role: The physician-leader ensures that the team is composed of all the personnel necessary to achieve the goal. The team will likely be interdisciplinary, depending on the problem to be addressed. One of the physician-leader's main roles is to ensure that the team understands its objective and avoids scope creep, going off into tangents that may be interesting but are irrelevant. The purpose of this team is to solve a focused problem as quickly and effectively as possible. In this regard, the physician-leader may be more directive than when leading other types of teams.

2. **Committee**: Hospitals are notorious for having committees to address systemic problems. These committees are often chaired by a physician with both physician and nonphysician members (e.g., quality and safety committee). For example, Johns Hopkins has committees that focus on ethics, critical care, documentation, hospital services, medical care evaluation, patient safety, quality, and risk management. These committees deal with systemic issues that are more complex and, typically, more impactful than issues addressed by problem-focused teams. Typically, these systemwide committees are ongoing, with team members holding positions for designated lengths of time, rolling off and on the committee in a staggered manner. These committees are more complex and require a broader view than the problem-focused teams. In fact, these committees often spin off problem-focused teams as a common method of achieving systemic progress.

   Physician-leader role: The physician-leader initially has an organizational role with a focus on creating, with the group, a committee charter consisting of the following (Barlow 2016):

   - Purpose
   - Objectives
   - Membership
   - Roles and responsibilities of membership
   - Meeting dates and times
   - Record keeping
   - Authority
   - Standard agenda

   Once a charter is established, the role of the physician-leader is to create the agenda, facilitate the meetings, assign tasks, and follow up on previously made assignments. The major responsibility of the physician-leader on this type of team is to provide the structure and cultivate the culture necessary to ensure that progress is being made toward accomplishing the committee's objectives, celebrating successes and stepping in when progress is languishing. In contrast to the problem-focused team, the committee's objectives are broader and more generalized, so the physician-leader is often less prescriptive.

3. **Management/administrative team**: These teams are typically composed of leaders from across the organization and exist to comprehensively manage large components of the organization or the entire organization itself. Examples of these teams are the Medical Executive Committee (MEC) and the senior executive team. The MEC is composed primarily of physicians and is responsible for creating and enacting policies and procedures to improve patient care and medical staff structure. The senior executive team typically includes the chief executive officer, chief operating officer, chief financial officer, chief medical officer, chief nursing officer, and so forth and exists to oversee the strategy and operations of the entire organization. Because of their expansive purpose, these teams are usually permanent. Many of the organization's committees will report into these teams. These are the most diverse and complex teams in any health care system, and managing these teams requires a breadth of skills and experiences that far exceeds those of other hospital roles.

   Physician-leader role: Leading such a diverse group of professionals to deal with complex and sophisticated issues requires the physician-leader to have extraordinary leadership skills and business acumen. Chief among these skills are strong interpersonal abilities, including being able to engage, collaborate, negotiate, compromise, and, at times, confront. Nowhere else will the power of influence be more valuable than when leading an administrative team. In addition, the physician-leader will need to be well versed in understanding operations, financials, interpreting data, and creating strategies to deal with both routine and unique problems associated with health care.

Creating a High-Performing Team

In all of the foregoing physician-led teams, physician-leaders can approach their roles as responsible taskmasters, coordinators, directors, or collaborators. Any of these behaviors will succeed in getting the job done. However, in order to create higher performing teams, more effort and structure is required. Is the effort required for driving a team from one that is average to one that is high performing warranted? Do high-performing teams really drive business results? According to several studies, they do. In fact, investors in start-ups often value the quality of the team and the interaction of the founding members more than the idea itself. For example, 90 percent of investors think the quality of the management team is the single most important nonfinancial factor when evaluating an initial public offering (IPO). This is why there is a 1.9 times increased likelihood of having *above-median financial performance* when the top team is working together toward a common vision (Keller and Meaney 2017).

In another study, 72 percent of 191 organizations surveyed said team performance has a positive, or extremely positive, impact on overall productivity. Priorities in these organizations were to have high-performing teams that enable business initiatives (42 percent) and drive results (36 percent) (Loew 2015).

The hallmark of a high-performing team resides in the *results* they attain and *how* they attain them. The measure of *results* is often lost when discussing teams, replaced by such things as absence of conflict, high empowerment, frequency of interaction, and other potentially irrelevant measures. Simply having a group of professionals together to discuss an issue or a problem does not ensure that the group will create the best possible solution, or any solution at all. Team results are a function of *productivity*, or what a team accomplishes, including quality and quantity of the outputs, and *vitality*, or how a team accomplishes its work, including team morale, engagement, and cohesiveness. Without both of these components, any team will be suboptimal (Figure 6.1; Kaiser, Overfield, and Kaplan 2010).

Vitality	High	High vitality Low productivity	High performing
	Low	Low vitality Low productivity	Low vitality High productivity
		Low	**High**
		Productivity	

Figure 6.1 Effectiveness of teams

Source: Kaiser, Overfield, and Kaplan (2010).

High-performing teams are characterized by *both* high levels of productivity and high levels of vitality. It is possible to have high levels of productivity *without* equally high levels of vitality (lower right quadrant). In these environments, the results are short-lived, and those who are able to leave the team eventually do so, leaving the lower-level performers behind. These teams often operate in a *sweatshop* environment, where task accomplishment trumps attention to people. Management of these teams is typically highly task focused, demanding, and punitive. The saying "the beatings will continue until morale improves" comes to mind. Ultimately, this environment leads to a team that continues to be low on vitality but then drifts into low productivity (lower left quadrant).

Similarly, it is possible to have high levels of vitality and lower levels of productivity (upper left quadrant). These environments are ones in which the goal of interpersonal relationships is promoted over that of getting results. In these environments, there is a notable absence of accountability and conflict. It is a *country club* environment in which people like each other and often refer to the family atmosphere of the workplace. The management of these teams is casual and relatively unstructured. These environments will ultimately lose people who are ambitious and recognize that the organization needs to have results in order to survive.

The high-performing team is one that balances a focus on results with a focus on people. These teams set stretch goals, encourage empowerment, hold people accountable, and provide rewards and incentives for extraordinary performance. These teams may also lose people, but they are usually those who do not want to put forth the effort required to be part of an elite group. Only a very small percentage of teams are high performing year over year. What makes the difference? Keep reading.

Case Study

The Happy but Unproductive Team

A physician-leader was asked to chair the quality committee in a midsize hospital in a large metropolitan area. The hospital had been having a threefold increase in central line-associated bloodstream infections (CLBSIs), and the committee was tasked with reviewing the cases involved to determine whether there were any patterns emerging. The membership of the quality committee had been predetermined by the CMO, and the physician-leader chair had not participated in the selection of committee members. The team was made up of a mixture of clinical and nonclinical members to ensure representation of all of the major service groups within the organization.

The charter of the committee was clearly to identify and eradicate factors contributing to the ongoing CLBSI crisis in the hospital. Time was of the essence because of both the impact to patients and the vulnerable accreditation of the hospital. The CMO requested an initial report from the team with identification of the problems and recommendations to address them, within a month's time. Under the direction of the committee chair, the committee began work on the problem.

An entire month went by without the CMO receiving a report. The physician-leader reassured her that a comprehensive report would be forthcoming. Another 2 weeks passed with still no report. By now, the CMO had independently interviewed some of the members, all of whom reported that they enjoyed being on the team and that the discussions they were having were engaging and important. To the person, they reported liking the chair and reported that the meetings were even fun. She could only wonder why she had not received the report. She asked us to consult with the team in order to better understand the team dynamics and learn what was causing the delay. There was now an increasingly greater sense of urgency to getting results.

Initially, we sat in on a meeting and quickly determined the problem. The chair had a high focus on relationships that permeated the group. The meeting had no agenda and began with a good deal of "catching up." The chair invited everyone to participate, and it was clear that there was little focus but much conversation. The chair was clearly more focused on being liked and creating a positive atmosphere than on getting results. Every possible rabbit was chased down every possible hole with no stone left unturned and no ideas that were considered out of bounds. While a committee member took copious notes, nothing was done with them to further the creation of a report. The meeting was more of a brainstorming session than a problem-solving meeting. This approach may have been appropriate in the first meeting, but definitely not 6 weeks into the process. The team was clearly a high-vitality, low-productivity team. It was operating like a country club, and it did not take a specialist in group dynamics to understand the problem.

We scheduled a meeting with the physician-leader chair to review our observations. The chair acknowledged that wanting people to like her and to get along well had been a lifelong characteristic. She was reluctant to impose any structure or agenda that might cause conflict. She also recognized that, as a result of this approach, the team had wandered away from its charter and failed to come up with a solution to the urgent CLBSI crisis. When we met with the chair and the CMO, the CMO gave the chair the option of receiving coaching or allowing someone else to take over as chair. The chair decided to step down instead of making the changes necessary to make the team a productive one. When a new physician-leader was selected, we were able to consult with her about how to give structure to team meetings and help the team become productive while not destroying morale in order to produce results. As a result, the new chair was able to focus the efforts of the group and provided the CMO with a comprehensive report within 2 weeks after beginning as chair. This was a good lesson for the CMO, namely, that getting results is the most important consideration when selecting staff to manage teams. Keeping a modicum of good morale in the process is important, but not as important as getting results. Succeeding at an important task creates the best morale and sense of satisfaction in the long run.

Characteristics of High-Performing Teams

High-performing teams do not occur accidentally. A number of very clear characteristics are required to transform from an assembled group of people to a high-performing team. Like most other successes in life, it begins with the leader! No surprise here. In our work with hundreds of organizations and thousands of leaders, we have identified the key elements required for making a team that is high performing. The model in Figure 6.2 demonstrates these characteristics (Figure 6.2).

Figure 6.2 Elements of a high-performing team

Leadership

Leadership of teams is an art much like leadership in general. It is ultimately the leader's responsibility to cultivate the climate, people, focus, communication, and execution necessary for teams to be highly effective. The manner in which a team leader produces these will vary greatly from one team to the next. The leader must understand the objectives and be able to decipher exactly what the team needs to succeed. Balance and adaptability are supreme virtues. The successful leader knows when to be passive and when to be assertive. The guidance of the team leader should always be sensed but rarely recognized.

The leaders of the high-performing teams make, or influence, most of the early decisions that set the tone for the team to function, interact, and execute. First and foremost, the leader creates a climate for the team members that is psychologically safe, encourages collaboration and problem-solving, and focuses on results. The leader creates a sense of urgency, transparency, and open communication with the premise that no idea is a bad idea. The leader is the choreographer and conductor, keeping the team focused, on-task, and motivated. The leader focuses more on inspiration than on driving specific behaviors. Nowhere is influence more needed than in leading a team toward high performance.

Leaders must demonstrate an encouragement to share the leadership when others on the team have the expertise required to solve a problem. In fact, the more leaders use influence over authority and power, the more others on the team take ownership and responsibility. The leader is ultimately responsible for team cohesion through the encouragement of behaviors that are consistent with the guidelines the team has created. Effective leaders both empower others and delegate regularly. The leader treats all team members equally and respectfully, setting the example for the team. The leader is equally responsible for the *deselection* of team members that are either no longer contributing or not adhering to the norms and standards created by the team. The leader is on guard for *social loafing* or underachieving members, as well as for those that are making extraordinary effort. Ultimately, the leader is responsible for resolving interpersonal conflicts that exist between members of the team and become escalated. Providing regular feedback is another significant role of the leader.

Climate

The climate of a high-performing team is one that is psychologically safe. All members feel important and appreciated, and their opinions are welcomed and respected. The primary objective in creating a healthy team climate is the formation of trust among individuals on the team. Without a trusting climate, the likelihood of having high levels of either vitality or productivity are significantly diminished. This trust extends to having radical candor among members, rigorously debating issues without denigrating individuals. A climate of mutual accountability exists in which any member can challenge the ideas, or work, of another in a spirit of cooperation and with a desire to achieve the best outcome. The team creates guidelines for expected individual behaviors to promote maximum cooperation and collaboration. These guidelines can range from completing assignments in a timely manner and at a suitable level to meeting attendance, to responding promptly to other team members. In some cases, confidentiality is expected to be observed.

In addition to creating an environment that is safe, high-performing teams also have environments in which performance, a sense of urgency, and a focus on results are paramount. This is the foundation for driving results that are high in quality, quantity, and timeliness. Without a commitment to results, team members may feel safe but not challenged, and the organization will suffer. This commitment to results also includes regularly bringing new ideas to the team from outside the team or the organization. By broadening the exposure of the team to new ideas, outcomes will be more creative and innovative. The team is not being formed to reinforce the status quo! Being on a high-performing team is a high honor and should be seen as such rather than simply additional work.

People

Second only to the selection of the leader, the selection of the people on the team will determine the success or failure of the endeavor. There has been significant research on the ideal size of teams as well as the type of people on the teams. With regard to size, the most effective teams are those between six and 10 members. Fewer than six may not result in enough diversity of thought on the team, and the team can be more prone to groupthink. With more than ten, it becomes increasingly challenging to get high levels of commitment from all members. On teams that are too large, accountability becomes more difficult, and the good workers perform a disproportionate amount of work, while those who are less assertive or ambitious can begin hiding in the shadows.

In health care, and particularly in problem-focused teams and committees, it is important for leaders to ensure that the team is comprised of members who possess the necessary expertise and represent the necessary areas to achieve the team goals. Leaders often inherit, or get promoted to head, teams that they had no choice in selecting. However, it is still the leader's responsibility to determine, over time, whether or not those inherited employees are the right ones for the work they have. The leader then needs to make decisions about who should be on the team, keeping some and deselecting others. As always, attaining results is the goal of the team. Selecting members for skill and skill potential is as important as or more important than picking members for personality.

Effective teams have a balance between specialization and diversity. Obviously, the more technically narrow the challenge, the more specialization that is required. However, having members on the team with a diversity of experiences that they bring to the team can be of great value. Absolutes in selecting team members are intelligence, strong problem-solving abilities, engagement, dependability, and commitment to the cause. Those with high emotional intelligence add the greatest value and are able to effectively negotiate difficult situations between peers.

There has been some research to suggest the self-selection of team members, assuming they meet previously established criteria, brings about better results than the selection of team members from a pool. By self-selecting, there is already a level of interest and, presumably, commitment. Contrary to what may seem logical, teams comprised, at least partially, of those who have never worked with each other before can bring about more innovative and creative ideas than those working with "that old gang of mine." High-performing teams are no place for those with personal agendas or divas who are overly self-promoting. As basketball great Michael Jordan said, "There is no i in team, but there is in win." High-performing teams are all about winning together.

Focus

The sine qua non of high-performing teams is focus, resulting from clarity of direction and expectations. First and foremost, the team needs to have a well-defined understanding of its purpose and central objective. Without this, any team will flounder and suboptimize attaining results. The team must have a clear understanding of what is to be achieved, what success looks like, the quality and quantity expected, time frames, and the resources required to get results. Although on the surface this may seem obvious, team after team fails either because of a lack of clarity or because of changing expectations along the way.

Once the objectives of the team are well understood, roles and responsibilities required of each team member need to be determined and assigned. The more meaningful and impactful the work, the greater the level of commitment, time, and energy team members will give. No one likes to work on tedious, mundane initiatives that add little value and take up time that could be given to more important work.

Team expectations are also related to goal-setting and priority-setting. The team must be results-oriented. The more involved the entire team becomes in translating strategy into action, setting goals, and determining together how to proceed and execute, the greater the chances of success. Having many talented members on the team can be a great benefit or a massive headache. One of the leader's greatest challenges is to get a team of highly talented, ambitious, and energetic people aligned and rowing in the same direction.

Communication

It is no surprise that effective communication is one of the essential elements of a high-performing team. Better communication is mentioned on every employee's list of how their organizations can be improved. On a high-performing team, the free flow of information is necessary for all team members to maintain focus, reduce redundant activities, and avoid missing any critical steps in managing a process. Communication begins with creating the climate and expectation of communication to foster freedom of expression, transparency, and inclusiveness. Establishing the vehicles and mechanisms for sharing information is a critical early decision that needs to be made to keep all team members well informed. In addition, there need to be good record-keeping processes such as concise meeting minutes or monthly updates that are easily accessible and regularly distributed in a timely manner.

One of the responsibilities of the leader is to encourage team members to consistently bring in fresh facts and information for the group to consider. At times, team members possess information that they may be reticent to share or may not realize is important. Other times, the information for solving a problem does not exist in the organization. By broadening the frame within which problems are presented while creating a culture that encourages team members to share ideas and acquire outside information, the team has a much better chance of arriving at solutions that are more effective, elegant, and longer lasting than by simply focusing on information already discussed or already existing in the organization. Sharing new information and fresh facts is another primary communication vehicle for group problem-solving.

A very important element of communication is effectively managing conflict. Being able to engage in rigorous debate and conflict is critical for team cohesiveness. To raise, and resolve, differences about issues more than about people, can bring people closer together. Suppressing conflict will undoubtedly create greater distance between team members and reduce trust. Even worse is allowing team members to engage in triangulation. Triangulation is the process of having a disagreement with one person and talking to a third person on the team about it, rather than the person with whom the problem exists. This kind of behavior contributes to gossip, innuendo, and the creation of a toxic environment. If two people cannot resolve an issue, they have the choice of escalating the issue to the team leader or even the entire team. It is ultimately the team leader's responsibility to ensure that all interpersonal issues are resolved. We will present a structure for having difficult conversations in Chapter 8.

Execution

Executing on any team requires having a process in place for translating concepts into action. High-performing teams create a process for translating initiatives into achievable goals (see Chapter 5). They understand what data they will need to achieve the goals and how to collect that data before crafting action plans to achieve the goals. In health care, as in any other industry, resource allocation is the foundation of the execution process and must be sufficient but not wasteful. The processes always include timelines, owners, level of quality and quantity required, and measurements to know when success has been achieved. Because creating an environment with a focus on results is critical, it is important for the leader to help the team seize on a few immediate performance-oriented tasks and goals. Accomplishment of these sets the stage for having a results-oriented climate.

In addition to having an execution process, high-performing teams have three very important group process principles to which they adhere:

1. **Collaboration**: High-performing teams all have collaborative problem-solving and joint decision making as central features for coming to decisions. This means the leader has the responsibility of harnessing all of the creativity and intelligence on the team to come to the best results possible. There can be no overreliance on just a few members, and there is no place for favoritism. In this regard, the leader is always encouraging, provoking, and challenging the individuals on the team to voice their opinions and share their expertise. Obviously, this can occur only in an environment where all members feel safe to voice their opinions, make mistakes without consequence and challenge each other's ideas respectfully.

2. **Accountability**: A requirement complementary to collaboration is accountability. For the most effective execution to take place, members must hold each other accountable for participation and for results. In order for the team to be truly high functioning, the leader cannot be the only one holding team members responsible. This will result in a hub-and-spoke type of management rather than shared leadership. The more responsibility that all of the team members take for individual and collective results, the higher the levels of productivity and vitality the team will experience.

3. **Incentives and rewards**: In addition to the honor of being identified as a member of a high-performing team working well to solve problems that are important to the enterprise, there are often other incentives and/or rewards associated with an extraordinary outcome. These may be in the form of a cash bonus, a promotion, a transfer, or public recognition. Not all work teams have incentives or rewards, but this should be determined at the outset of the project. Typically, the more important and complex the problem that the team is trying to solve, the greater the postwork reward. To the extent possible, this becomes something the entire team can experience. In particular, the leader must utilize the motivating advantage of promoting recognition, rewards, and positive feedback.

The Psychology of Teams

Understanding the elements of a high-performing team and understanding team dynamics are related, but different. Although each team is different in regard to personalities, expectations, and leadership, there are some team dynamics that are common to all teams. In particular, the stages of group development, as determined by Bruce Tuckman, are a well-known and accepted model of group formation (Tuckman 1965). Tuckman's research determined that as groups are forming, they go through four stages on the path to performing. Although groups can stall out at any point in time, high-performing groups successfully negotiate each stage. The stages include the following:

Forming: In the initial stages, the members of the group are getting to know one another and learning about the purpose of convening, the goals, opportunities, and challenges in front of them. At this stage, members are on their best behavior and are operating independently as they go through an orientation process. Discussion centers on defining the scope and scale of the project.

Storming: As the group begin to work together, they begin to recognize differences and size up each other as to competence, capability, working style, and trustworthiness. The ability to express these differences and successfully resolve conflict determines the degree to which both intimacy and trust can be developed. Some groups do not get beyond this stage because a high degree of trust is not created, owing to either unexpressed differences, in which members move away from each other, or more destructive conflict, in which power becomes more important than goal accomplishment. It takes an adept leader to help the team develop an environment in which disagreements can be openly expressed without becoming personal.

Norming: It is at this stage that team members have developed effective means for dealing with conflict and differences so that they can begin taking responsibility for the success of the team's goals. Team members begin accepting others as they are and working together to create solutions to the challenges they face. Clarity of roles and responsibilities helps structure the team and create a sense of cohesiveness and alignment.

Performing: In Tuckman's final phase, with group norms and roles established, group members start focusing on their common goals. Team members are able to work well together or autonomously, as the situation requires. The team begins achieving success toward the end state, and people share both their successes and failures as a team.

Adjourning: Tuckman later added this phase, indicating that the team had completed the task and begins to break up. It is at this stage that celebrations, rewards, and recognition take place.

At the initial meeting, the leader needs to review with the team the expected phases of group development. Individuals and teams perform better when they know what to expect. It is particularly important to *normalize* the storming stage so team members recognize that having, and constructively voicing, disagreements is necessary for intimacy and relationship development.

The Physician-Leader: Challenges and Opportunities

It should be clear by now that the role of a physician-leader in managing teams is broad, complex, and different from managing a clinical practice. Depending on the type of team being led, the physician-leader will recognize some differences from clinical practice and management including the following:

- The focus of attention (patient vs. patients/organization)
- The physician's role (expert vs. facilitator/collaborator/choreographer)
- The members of the group (clinical vs. clinical/administrative)
- The time frame for results (short-term to longer-term)
- Managing the group (physician-centric hub and spoke vs. shared leadership)

One challenge specific to physicians leading teams is the need to step out of the perspective of their own specialty. Physician-leaders at an organizational level must be able to look at each situation through an organizational lens. This is particularly difficult for new physician-leaders who have grown up viewing the world from an internal medicine, general surgery, anesthesia or other specialty perspective. As with any business, the best physician-leaders are able to put themselves in the shoes of others.

As discussed in Chapter 3, *agreeableness* is often found in physicians. While agreeableness can nurture collaboration in a team, it can also impede the maturation of the team with regard to respectful conflict and confrontation. Healthy confrontation is paramount in achieving superlative team results. Overreliance on agreeableness can also lead to prolonged and potentially flawed team decision making that is disproportionately biased toward creating consensus. Consensus decision making is often but not always the most effective method.

Extraversion is another common personality characteristic of physicians. This can also create some challenges in leading highly effective teams. It can result in the physician-leader being overly vocal and directive in the team setting. Instead of functioning as facilitator and choreographer, the physician-leader can easily fall into the old clinical standard of the physician at the center of the discussion and decision making.

Earlier, we discussed the fact that physicians can have a profound impact on any team because of the respect and assumption of expertise that they are afforded by others in health care. This advantage also creates disadvantages for the physician-leader and may compound the dangers of extraversion. Great care must be taken to avoid suboptimizing team performance. If a physician-leader speaks too often, too early, or too definitively, it may suppress ideas from the team, predetermine decisions, and eliminate productive confrontation. Because of the traditional physician role in health care, the team may be predisposed to interpret the physician-leader's input as doctrine or mandate. The adept physician-leader will be aware of this and navigate this challenge by being intentional with the quantity, content, and tone of his or her participation while working to cultivate the aforementioned qualities of high-performing teams.

Coach's Corner

Leaders cannot lead without teams, and highly effective leaders achieve results through high-performing teams. Physician-leaders will be asked to lead many different types of teams. The best physician-leaders will adapt their leadership perspective and style to each type of team in order to achieve teams that are strong in both productivity and vitality.

1. **Describe the difference between leading a clinical team and an administrative team**
   - Using your experience and the information in this book, write down the key components of how clinical teams function versus how administrative teams function. Identify leadership strategies that would be effective for both types of teams as opposed to strategies that would be more effective for only one type of team.

2. **Historically, how do you lead teams?**
   - Reflect on teams that you have led in the past. What strengths and weaknesses did you bring to those teams? What would you have done differently in hindsight? Identify the differences in approach that you should bring to future team-leading roles.

3. **Identify a role model**
   - We have all been a part of a highly effective team at some point in our careers. Choose a role model in team leadership, and identify the specific behaviors they exhibit that are different from your natural behaviors. Be mindful of these behaviors as you work on becoming a more effective team leader.

References

Angood, P. May–June, 2014. "The Value of Physician Leadership." *Physician Executive* 40, no. 3, p. 6.

Barlow, J. 2016. *How to Write a Charter for a Committee.* Board Effect. https://www.boardeffect.com/blog/how-to-write-a-charter-for-a-committee (accessed May 2, 2019).

Edmonson, A. December, 2015. "The Kinds of Teams Healthcare Needs." *Harvard Business Review: Leadership.* https://hbr.org/2015/12/the-kinds-of-teams-health-care-needs (accessed December 27, 2018).

Fibuch, E., and A. Ahmed. March, 2018. "Bringing Value: Build a Functional Leadership Team." *American Association for Physician Leadership.* https://www.physicianleaders.org/news/bringing-value-build-a-functional-leadership-team (accessed December 27, 2018).

Kaiser, R.B., D.V. Overfield, and R.E. Kaplan. 2010. *Leadership Versatility Index.* Greensboro, NC: Kaplan DeVries Inc.

Keller, S., and M. Meaney. 2017. *Leading Organization: Ten Timeless Truths*, New York, NY: Bloomsbury.

Loew, L. April, 2015. "High-Performance Teams: A Crucial Differentiator of Business Performance." *Training.* https://trainingmag.com/high-performance-teams-crucial-differentiator-business-performance (accessed December 29, 2018).

Tuckman, B.W. 1965. "Developmental Sequence in Small Groups." *Psychological Bulletin* 63, no. 6, pp. 384–99.

Weir, K. September, 2018. "What Makes Teams Work?" *Monitor on Psychology* 49, no. 8, pp. 47–54.

Wood, D. April, 2012. "Collaborative Healthcare Teams a Growing Success Story." *Healthcare News.* https://www.amnhealthcare.com/latest-healthcare-news/collaborative-healthcare-teams-growing-success-story (accessed December 27, 2018).

CHAPTER 7

Delegation: Maximizing Leadership Impact

In clinical practice, the wise and efficient physician delegates many duties to nurses, medical assistants, and other staff because of time constraints. Obviously, physicians cannot do everything for their patients, nor is it desirable. Because the current primary care system is inefficient and overstretched, primary care physicians, sometimes seeing over 40 patients per day, are hard-pressed to handle patients' needs without cutting corners (Lichtenstein et al. 2015). This stretching of physicians to do more and more is a major contributor to the 46 percent of physicians suffering from burnout (Schattner 2012). Whether by design, or out of necessity, physicians have learned how to delegate in clinical settings. They perform better and enjoy the work more.

An important distinction of typical clinical delegation is that it often does not entail true delegation of responsibility and decision making. When delegating to nurses and medical assistants, the tasks being delegated are often important but do not require high-level decision making. An example of this is medication administration. In contrast, delegation to an advanced practice provider does involve transferring some responsibility and decision making. Research on geriatric patient care has determined that delegation to nonphysician providers is associated with a higher quality of care for geriatric conditions in community practices (Abrams 2013). Indeed, some physicians have become partially or totally comfortable delegating decision making to advanced practice providers, but many physicians still struggle with giving up control and responsibility. Effective delegation for physician-leaders requires embracing this next level of delegation.

Compared with its significance in a clinical role, delegation in a leadership role is equally critical, in a slightly different way. In a clinical setting, many tasks are delegated because there is more work to do than time or resources allow. The same holds true in physician-leadership roles. However, there are clearly differences because of the primary focus for physician-leaders. Although patient care or quality may be behind the need to delegate, for the physician-leader this relationship is a much more distant one, often with several layers between the physician and the patient. In physician-leadership roles, the focus is on the function, service line, or organization. The higher the physician-leader rises in the organization, the more the focus will shift from frontline operations to system operations, policy, and strategy. Clearly, patient safety and quality can still be the areas of focus, but at the system or policy level rather than at the individual patient level.

In leadership roles, the physician is often working with nonphysicians and even nonclinicians. In fact, many health care leadership roles at the administrative levels involve mostly nonclinicians (e.g., finance, information technology, medical records, facilities, marketing). The physician-leader may be a part of an interdisciplinary team or leading one. When leading the team, the physician-leader may have some choice as to the talent and skills that are on the team. Unlike the clinical setting, the roles on the team are more varied and have greater specialization of skills.

Why Delegate?

The most obvious question to be answered by physician-leaders is, why delegate those things that the physician-leaders may be qualified to do themselves and may even do better? The obvious answer is limited bandwidth. It has been said that "you can do anything, but not everything." It is important to do that which is of high priority and not try to do all there is to do. Stephen Covey noted that the urgent can often undermine the important. One of the early lessons physician-leaders must learn is that in order to accomplish the goals of the larger organization, there is more work to be done than any one person can, or should, do. In addition, there are skills and capabilities that others possess that may be better suited for some of the work. We have identified four major reasons the physician-leader must learn to delegate.

1. **Productivity**: Any health care organization has multiple initiatives going on simultaneously. The organization functions like one big flywheel, always moving and waiting for no one. The most effective organizations recognize that it requires a team to undertake all of the work in order to get ahead of, or even keep up with, the demands of multiple constituents. The most effective physician-leaders understand the necessity of delegating. At its core, delegation makes possible getting more work accomplished through others than any one person could manage alone in the time allotted. As measured by volume of work, productivity is one measure of a high-performing organization.

2. **Impact:** In order to deliver the highest value contribution, physician-leaders need to focus on those issues that are the most important, not just the most urgent. *Effective* delegation is about maximizing impact. This requires physician-leaders to differentiate the work they should do from what should be delegated. It also requires them to be selective with regard to whom work is delegated. The most important work with the highest impact should be undertaken by either the physician-leader themselves or someone who has a full grasp of the items being delegated. The concept of maximizing impact is often referred to in the clinical setting as having staff work at *the top of their license*. In other words, each person must focus on activities at the high end of what their training or license allows, avoiding the busy work that a lesser trained individual could accomplish. We have referred to the physician-leader in many ways as the conductor of an orchestra. Although the conductor may have once been a violinist or other musician, the most beautiful music is created only if the conductor focuses on leading and coordinating the various musicians as opposed to stepping in and playing the violin. Thus is the challenge for physician-leaders.

3. **Development:** The growth and development of the leader's staff is always a high priority for an effective leader. The best physician-leaders regularly look for opportunities to increase both the depth and the breadth of their subordinates for succession planning and increasing organizational effectiveness. Sending staff to workshops and additional education are ways of increasing staff capabilities. However, on-the-job development is more directly related to the organization and is practical and cost-effective as a way to develop staff. Providing growth opportunities through delegation of stretch assignments

gives staff members the opportunity to increase their capabilities under the supervision of a supportive manager. Being supportive means, at least in part, both accepting and tolerating failure. Stretch assignments are meant to expand the limits of staff capability. Despite appropriate oversight, errors will occur. The best learning will result from these failures. The key for the leader is to avoid the so-called *fatal* errors and provide positive reinforcement for staff when they do fail as long as they are not committing the same mistakes repeatedly.

4. **Creating Brain Space**: Finally, the physician-leader is freeing up time for thinking about higher-order issues by delegating effectively. Such issues may include organizational planning, talent development, innovation, trends in health care, policy reviews, or a host of any other items that have a broad impact on the organization and warrant time to consider, study, and plan. When the physician-leader stays mired in details that others could handle, there is no time to meet the expectations that led to the physician-leader being promoted into the role. This concept is an underappreciated core component of leadership. Strategy development and leading, in general, requires thought, not just action. Too many leaders fail to create the brain space necessary to think and thereby improve both themselves and their organizations.

Case Study

Assign or Perish

The Chair of the Pediatric Department of a large academic medical center was balancing clinical practice with the demands of chair responsibilities. New in her role, she complained about not having enough hours in the day to get all of her work completed. She found herself arriving each morning before the other physicians arrived and leaving in the evening after all other staff had been long gone. In addition, she realized she had begun coming in on Saturdays to get paperwork completed and even answering e-mails from home on Sundays. When she had accepted the position, she had done so with much enthusiasm and had great plans for improvements that could be made to patient care, education, and research. Now, 6 months into the role, she was considering whether she should return exclusively to clinical practice. She had that conversation with her boss, the Dean of the School of Medicine, letting him know of her dilemma. The Dean suggested that working with an executive coach might help her sort through the issues and provide her with alternatives that could make her schedule more balanced and her workload more tolerable.

When we met with the new physician-leader, we were impressed with her passion, her vision, and her level of engagement. We were also aware that she was fatigued and on the front end of feeling defeated because of the load she was carrying. As a first step, we conducted, with her encouragement, a full personality evaluation to determine whether any personality dynamics could be impacting her work style.

The results of the evaluation were striking. Like most pediatricians, she had a high level of *agreeableness*. She clearly valued relationships and regularly put relationship development above task accomplishment. She was compassionate, cooperative, and inclusive. She also had an exceedingly high level of *conscientiousness*. She was highly disciplined, detail oriented, and highly organized. She was a perfectionist on steroids. This combination of having a high sensitivity to the demands she might ask of others with her strong penchant for having everything done as flawlessly as possible resulted in her sense of great pressure to do everything herself, rather than delegate any tasks.

She was missing two key requisites for becoming an effective physician-leader: differentiating between what is truly important from what seems urgent but is not very important and relying on her team to help her through effective delegation. We began helping her develop a process by which all of the many tasks she had could be triaged into one of three categories: tasks that must be done now, tasks that can wait until later, and tasks that do not need to be done at all. We further helped her recognize that, in order to succeed, she would have to trust her staff and be willing to delegate a substantial amount of her work. We helped her see that her perfectionism had more to do with the unrealistic expectations she had of herself than the degree to which tasks needed to be done flawlessly or immediately. She readily embraced our counsel and began to triage and delegate. Her new approach proceeded by fits and starts, but she was persistent. We checked back with her in 3 months and found a new person. Her ability to let go of her perfectionism and trust others to help her had paid massive dividends. She was again able to enjoy her clinical practice along with her administrative duties. She was working reasonable hours and had stopped coming in every weekend. Ultimately, she was pleased that she had taken on the role and was beginning to see good progress on the problems she had sought to improve.

Why Delegating Is Difficult: Understanding Your Delegation Style

In spite of physician-leaders grasping the importance of delegation, we have identified some prevalent management styles that can undermine effective delegation. Even with the physician-leaders' best intentions, their preexisting personality and relationship formation impact their delegation style. We have identified three dysfunctional delegation styles.

The Micromanager: A physician's training requires high levels of attention to detail and the assumption of full responsibility for patient outcomes. Conscientiousness and micromanaging can go hand in hand. The micromanaging physician-leader may delegate but continue to hover, push, redo work, and make the life of their staff very difficult. This occurs because of the following:

- Trust: Physician-leaders may not trust those to whom they are delegating. This typically is more about the physician-leader being concerned about outcomes than about the capabilities of the individuals to whom they are delegating. It is also related to the physician being required to manage all aspects of patient care in the clinical arena. This same sense of responsibility can interfere with trusting others to complete assignments. When physician-leaders do not trust the staff to complete delegated work, they need to ask themselves one of three questions:

1. Do they have the right people under them? If not, should they restructure to get the right people in the right positions?

2. Do the people under them have the right skill set? If not, do they need to provide them with additional training to be effective?

3. Do they need to grow in their intrinsic ability to trust? If so, they may need to ask themselves what is behind their difficulty in trusting.

No one likes to have someone constantly looking over his or her shoulders and managing every step. It is toxic for the morale and for productivity. Distrusting your staff will lead to good people leaving.

- Control: Equally destructive effects of having a lack of trust flow from the physician-leader who must control all aspects of what is delegated. This is another holdover from clinical practice in which many physicians feel the need to be in full control of patient treatment. By keeping all aspects of a patient's care under his or her control, the physician can take greater comfort in a positive outcome. As a physician-leader, this same level of managing all aspects of what is delegated is ineffective, at best, and detrimental to both staff and ultimate outcomes, at worst. Similar to the clinical setting, another peril that physician-leaders face in this arena is maintaining control by only delegating transactional tasks as opposed to more complex projects that require some delegation of authority and decision making. Inability to delegate the latter will result in suboptimal organizational performance.

- Perfectionism: Physician mistakes in clinical practice can have dire consequences, including bad patient outcomes, medical liability, or even loss of the physician's license. In perhaps no other profession is the focus on "measuring twice and cutting once" more prevalent than in the medical profession. As a result, physicians become perfectionists, if they are not already predisposed. The same perfectionism is rarely required in the world of organizational life, and it can even interfere with productivity, impact, and morale. It becomes important for the physician-leader to spend time differentiating between those rare issues that require a high level of perfection and those that do not. Being perfectionistic on all matters results in analysis paralysis and can bring the organization to a halt. Although it is important to have standards for what is delegated, the physician-leader needs to be realistic in his or her demands, balancing the quality of work with the outcomes needed.

The Abdicator: It is very common in leadership practice to hear about the importance of "empowering" others to do the work they have been assigned. The principle behind empowerment is that people need to have authority commensurate with responsibility. In other words, when people are delegated work and given guidelines on the level of quality and time lines needed, they should be able to get the work completed in a manner consistent with their particular work style. However, for some leaders, empowerment means throwing work "over the fence" and not being involved in any subsequent measure. In short, their style is benign neglect. The new physician-leader, often unaccustomed to delegating in an administrative sphere, can inadvertently abdicate. This is often because of a lack of management training and/or not having a process in place. Interestingly, benign-neglect leaders are often the ones that talk about their "great staff," primarily because they do not have to do much work! Being an absent leader is every bit as harmful as being one that is overinvolved. It impacts staff morale and erodes the leader's credibility. We have identified three primary reasons for this abdication of responsibility.

- Overbooked: In particular, new physician-leaders often have difficulty declining requests for meetings, assignments, or involvement on committees. They may not have the experience to differentiate between those requests to which they should commit and those they could deal with by delegating or not accepting altogether. As a result, their full schedule interferes with the oversight of delegated assignments. Learning how to say "no" appropriately is a skill most leaders must learn early in their careers.
- Fear of interfering: Physician-leaders are not exempt from wanting to be liked. In fact, being liked, alongside with being respected, are good leadership foundations. However, when their need to be liked keeps them from getting involved for fear of hurting feelings or being seen as overmanaging, it will cause problems with both productivity

and morale. Ultimately, it is a failure to create healthy boundaries when the physician-leader wants to be more of a friend than a manager. Such leaders lose the respect of their staff. Strong people want ongoing involvement with their leader and consider it a vote of confidence. On the other hand, inattentive leaders create weaker staff.

- Inattention to detail: Periodically (although likely rare as physicians are known to be high in conscientiousness), it is the case that the physician-leader is highly conceptual and not detail oriented. These leaders are more likely to see the big picture and look at systems rather than focus on tactics. Once they have a broad understanding of a problem or issue, they can become bored with implementation. Work coming from these physician-leaders may be more strategic but is less likely to be flush with details. This approach can work when the physician-leader is surrounded by detail-oriented, self-managing staff. However, if the final product is not scrutinized after it is delegated, there may be organizational consequences that are unpleasant.

The Waffler: This delegation style is characterized by the physician-leader regularly changing directions, baffling staff, and creating havoc. In one privately held organization with which we consult, the CEO/founder will reach agreement with his staff on a particular direction or set of objectives on which to focus their work. The staff will begin working on the objectives outlined by the CEO. The staff will hold subsequent update meetings, engage vendors, and begin making decisions. However, not uncommonly, the CEO, who is often taking time off, will helicopter back in to let the staff know either that he has changed his mind on the subject or that their work is substandard and he wants to go in a different direction. Needless to say, this undermines the staff and undercuts their authority to make decisions. Morale is always low, and staff have learned not to begin working on something until the CEO has mentioned several times that he wants to go in a particular direction without wavering. Talk about a loss of productivity!

These delegators tend to be plagued by insecurity. They are constantly questioning their own decisions and regularly rethinking decisions they have previously made. In addition, they are often characterized by the "shiny new object" syndrome, in which they are always believing that a better idea is "out there." As a result, they have difficulty committing to a course of action. They can also be victims of the "last-in" syndrome. Similar to attraction to the "shiny new object," the leader will gravitate to the opinions of the last individual to whom they spoke (usually outside the company) and make decisions based on that conversation. Obviously, this is a vicious cycle because there is always the next "last-in" person's opinion to consider. Of the three dysfunctional delegators, the helicopter is the least predictable and most destructive. Such unpredictability keeps staff constantly off balance and on edge.

Regardless of what kind of dysfunctional delegation is represented, such physician-leaders seriously suboptimize their staff. They also risk either slowing down progress (as in the case of the micromanager), producing lower quality results (the abdicator), or frustrating their organizations while *both* slowing down progress and producing suboptimal results (the waffler). Learning to become an effective delegator is a companion skill to creating a vision (Chapter 5) and developing a high-performing team (Chapter 6).

Effective Delegation: Creating a Process

The biggest challenges of new physician-leaders are to: (1) differentiate issues with regard to complexity and impact; (2) understand the capabilities of their staff; (3) put a process in place to delegate effectively; (4) create accountability. We have found that having a process not only ensures that work gets done, but that the physician-leader is focusing time and effort on the right kind of issues and has a rationale for those things that are delegated. Keep in mind that advantages to effective delegation include creating both great outcomes and brain space for the physician-leader. Effective delegation is systematic and stepwise, providing the mechanism by which the physician-leader can effectively manage the organization.

Differentiating issues by establishing beachheads: Not all issues are alike. In the course of a day, week, or month, numerous requests cross the desk of physician-leaders. New physician-leaders tend to say "yes" too often because they do not have the experience to effectively determine those requests in which they should be involved, those they can delegate, or those that do not need to be dealt with at all. This process is simply an-other application of the skill of triage, with which physicians are already adept.

Early in their positions, physician-leaders need to establish *beachheads* pertaining to their, and their team's, availability to be involved in orga-nizational initiatives. These beachheads are the parameters defining the kinds of initiatives in which they will, and will not, be involved. It is important to broadcast these parameters to the organization. An enor-mous amount of time is wasted in organizational meetings that are often unnecessary, involve people not directly related to the issue, and do not have an agenda or a plan. In a survey of 182 executives, researchers found that executives spend an average of nearly 23 hours per week in meet-ings. Here are some staggering statistics about the impact of meetings and e-mails on the time of organization leaders (Chignell 2019; Perlow, Hadley, and Eun 2017).

- 65 percent of managers believe meetings keep them from complet-ing their own work
- 71 percent believe meetings are unproductive and inefficient
- 64 percent said that meetings come at the expense of deep thinking
- 62 percent said meetings miss opportunities to bring the team closer together
- Dysfunctional meeting behaviors have been associated with lower levels of market share, innovation, and employment stability
- A typical corporate employee receives about 110 e-mail messages daily
- The average number of *legitimate* corporate e-mails received daily is 62
- Of the legitimate e-mails, only a small number are *directly related* to the receiver

These statistics point to the alarming truth that an incredible amount of time and productivity is lost sitting in meetings that are poorly con-ceived, have the wrong invitees, and are poorly run, resulting in equally poor outcomes. More time is lost in reading and responding to unneces-sary e-mails. Thus, when considering all of the requests that will be made of physician-leaders, they need to make certain that each one really needs attention from them or their staff and justifies the expenditure of time and energy required. Surprisingly, this is the first prerequisite in creating a delegation process. The less physician-leaders have to do or delegate, the more time there is available for them and their staffs to work on more important issues. In this respect, physician-leaders become the gatekeepers for their areas of responsibility.

Gatekeeping: Assuming the request of the physician-leader crosses the threshold of being warranted, requests typically fall into four categories. We have found that the importance and uniqueness of the request assists physician-leaders in determining whether or not the request actually needs their attention.

- Information: These requests are usually information-only requests. As such, they are simple and do not require much time or energy on the part of the recipient. Unless the information is confidential or known only to the physician-leader, it can usually be delegated. In the event that you, or your staff, are on a large distribution list for communication, request the senders to delete you from the list unless you have something specific to contribute.

- Involvement: With involvement, the expertise or wise counsel of the physician-leader or their subordinates is being requested in the form of being involved on a standing committee or task force. Caution! When there is a request for you, or your staff, to be on a committee or task force, resist the urge if possible. Unless truly warranted, these are incredibly low-productivity time killers. At the least, request an agenda to review before accepting any invitations.

- Problem-solving: Almost universally, these requests need to have the attention of the physician-leaders or their staffs. However, as noted previously, ensure that you are not simply part of a distribution list and that there is specificity with regard to the request.

- Crisis: Typically, the physician-leader needs to be involved in these requests. They are very specific and short term. The role of the physician-leader is very clear. Requests of this sort often come from senior leaders in the organization, and participation is expected.

Understanding Talent: Matching Requests with Capabilities

Once requests have been appropriately sorted and the physician-leader has determined which of the requests can be delegated (versus doing or discarding), the next step is to determine to whom the request/work should be delegated. The gating process needs to include how complex the work is, the impact of the work, and the urgency of the request. These are prerequisites in determining to whom the work should go. On any staff, leaders typically have a "go-to" person—that person who is consistently reliable, gets work completed at a high level and in a timely manner. That is the good news. The downside to delegating to the go-to person is that he or she becomes inundated with requests, and the workload in the organization becomes skewed, with less reliable or lesser known staff doing less work. Conducting a review of the capabilities of the staff to consider to whom requests should be given saves time and increases productivity. In addition, when reflecting on developing staff, it is often the case that you will want to delegate stretch assignments to them, in order to help them in their professional growth. We have found that having a delegation matrix (Figure 7.1) can be helpful to determine to whom you want to delegate (Beard and Weiss 2017).

		Delegation matrix	
Work difficulty	**Complex**	Delegate for growth	**Delegate critical and difficult**
	Simple	Delegate simple or routine	Do not delegate
		Adequate or newer/high potential	**Strong, well developed**
		Strength of skillset	

Figure 7.1 Delegation matrix

Source: Beard and Weiss (2017).

In this matrix, the leader classifies the staff according to the strength of their skill set. Work requests are classified according to the difficulty or criticality. The intersection of these variables determines to whom requests are delegated. In this respect, delegation becomes intentional rather than haphazard. The process ensures that the work will be undertaken by those with capabilities commensurate with the request. It also ensures that the work will be completed at a level that satisfies the request. This process is a tool for physician-leaders to multiply their impact in the organization, rather than simply being productive.

Delegation Tools for Results

At this point, the physician-leader has vetted the request, identified to whom the request should be assigned, and made the assignment. All done, right? Well, not quite done yet. Being intentional about vetting and assigning are necessary preconditions for success. Now the work begins. Being clear about expectations for outcomes is equally important. The Levinson Institute has created a simple, but powerful, way to think about delegation expectations. It believes that accountability must be clearly defined and has developed a formula for accountability (Kraines 2001):

$$\text{Accountability} = Q + Q + T/R$$

In this formula, Accountability is the sum total of quality, quantity, timeliness, and the resources required to complete the assignment. Accountability is the responsibility of individuals to complete the tasks they are assigned in a timely manner and with the expected results. This definition requires two predetermined practices. First, individuals must be given *clarity* with regard to the expectations they are expected to meet. Second, individuals must be given the *authority* commensurate with the responsibilities they have been assigned. Using this approach provides the specifics with regard to the physician-leader's expectations for the work being assigned. This provides a scorecard of sorts for evaluating the completeness of the final work product.

Quality: This relates to both fully completing the work and maximizing the intended *impact* of the results. Quality always includes significant attention to detail, correctness, accuracy, and excellence in the final product. Producing a high-quality work product also includes seeking the input of other experts, ensuring that the work follows well-established workplace principles, and identifying all of the needs that must be satisfied in completing the task. Questions to ask include the following: (1) Have the right people been included in the final review? (2) Does everyone have the information required to make decisions about the outcome? (3) Has a venue been established for reviewing and presenting the work? (4) Have adequate communication channels been established to communicate about work products to selected audiences? Missing any one of these characteristics suboptimizes the final work product.

Quantity: As it would seem to imply, quantity is how much, or how many, of the final products are required in order to consider the assignment completed. Quantity is also the degree to which the completion of a task fulfills its intent. Does completing 50 percent of the paperwork fulfill the expectation of task accomplishment? By checking half of the patients on rounds will the clinician have satisfied the requirement for managing patient quality or safety? When work is assigned, built into the front end of the task should be clear specifications with regard to the amount or degree of task completion that satisfies the intent of the assignment. It cannot be assumed that individuals to whom tasks are assigned will automatically know exactly what is required for successful task completion.

Timeliness: Establishing dates and times for reviewing milestones of the work process needs to be done up front. Creating and scheduling a cadence of review updates is required. Another up-front requirement is determining if there are intermediate milestones that must be met and what conditions require escalation for reviewing problems. Also, a date for the final presentation of the work product must be established.

Resources: Physician-leaders are responsible for ensuring that those to whom they have delegated the work have the resources to get the work completed in a satisfactory manner. This usually involves a discussion between the physician-leader and the staff person to whom the work has been assigned. It makes little sense to assign an important initiative and handcuff the individual doing the work because the right resources have not been identified and allocated. Resources include financial as well as human resources. If applicable, has a budget been established for completion of the project or product? It is important to pinpoint other organizational functions that will be impacted in the accomplishment of the task and other people that will need to be notified to secure their support.

Incentives: Most delegated assignments are part of the day-to-day work and a routine part of the job. However, there are assignments that are so large, important, or long-lasting that when they are assigned, there is a carrot offered to be received at the completion of the assignment. An example of such a situation would be that of offering a carrot for taking the assignment to be on a merger integration team for a newly acquired company. This merger integration work would be done in addition to their "day job." As such, the individual conducting the work will be involved at nights and on weekends for a period of time until the integration is completed. A financial reward or promotional assignment may be the carrot at the end of the project. Typically, these kinds of rewards are for assignments that go above and beyond the individual's routine work and temporarily extend his/her job description considerably, on behalf of helping the company.

These delegation tools are effective only inasmuch as they are adhered to by the manager. It is our experience that when projects fail, it is usually the result of poor up-front delegation requirements being established (QQT/R) and poor follow-up. The discipline of incorporating this process into delegation will better ensure that work will be accomplished as intended.

What You Can Never Delegate

There are some things physician-leaders can never delegate, particularly as they move into administrative roles. These are items or issues that have some level of confidentiality associated with them. The higher physician-leaders rise in an organization, the more they are privy to information that is not available to the overall organization. Typically, the dissemination of this information requires discretion.

Confidential workplace information usually falls into one of three areas: employee information, management information, and business information (Halpern 2015).

- Employee information includes confidentiality associated with the sharing of personal identifiers. In addition, employees' medical and disability information must be kept confidential and has limited access on a "need-to-know" basis.

- Management information includes information related to employee relations issues: disciplinary actions, impending layoffs, terminations, and workplace investigations.
- Business information refers to "proprietary information" or "trade secrets." This is information not generally known to the public or available to competitors. Business information can also include pending acquisitions or the launch of new products and services.

Using confidential information indiscriminately or leaking it, inadvertently or otherwise, can be a disciplinary matter and have serious consequences, including loss of position or personal liability exposure. Similar to doctor–patient confidentiality, confidentiality at the organizational level can be breached only when it is determined that significant harm may result if the information is not disclosed to the right person. There is typically a very narrow interpretation of when a breach is justified and on whose authority the interpretation rests. It is always better to be conservative in dealing with such issues.

Coach's Corner

Leadership is achieving results through others. Strong leadership requires aligning the efforts of others so that the product is not simply additive but synergistic. Effective delegation is not simply tasking others with work. The delegation process and tactics outlined in this chapter provide the foundation of strong leadership.

1. **Identify your delegation style**
   - Reflect on your personal delegation style. Do you suffer from characteristics of the Micromanager, the Abdicator, or the Waffler? Identify specific actions you can take to improve your delegation style.
2. **Focus on your delegation process**
   - Apply the delegation matrix and its prerequisites to your delegation process. Create an action plan to develop the process components that you are not currently employing effectively.

References

Abrams, L. February, 2013. "To Love Medicine Again, Physicians Need to Delegate." *Health*. https://www.theatlantic.com/health/archive/2013/02/to-love-medicine-again-physicians-need-to-delegate/272782 (accessed January 21, 2019)

Beard, M., and A. Weiss, A. 2017. *The DNA of Leadership: Creating Healthy Leaders and Vibrant Organizations.* New York, NY: Business Expert Press.

Chignell, B. January, 2019. "How to Manage Email Overload at Work." *CIPHR*. https://www.ciphr.com/advice/email-overload/ (accessed May 2, 2019).

Halpern, J. October, 2015. "Why Is Confidentiality Important?" *Jules Halpern Associates LLC News and Articles.* https://www.halpernadvisors.com/category/restrictive-covenants (accessed January 24, 2019).

Kraines, G. 2001. *Accountability Leadership: How to Strengthen Productivity through Sound Managerial Leadership.* Pompton Plaines, NJ: The Career Press.

Lichtenstein, B.J., D.B. Reuben, A.S. Karlamangla, W. Han, C.P. Roth, N.S. Wenger. October, 2015. "The Effect of Physician Delegation to Other Health Care Providers on the Quality of Care for Geriatric Conditions." *Journal of the American Geriatric Society* 63, no. 10, pp. 2164–170. https://www.ncbi.nlm.nih.gov/pmc/articles/PMC4762652 (accessed January 21, 2019).

Perlow, L., C.N. Hadley, and E. Eun. July–August, 2017. "Stop the Meeting Madness." *Harvard Business Review*, pp. 62–69. https://hbr.org/2017/07/stop-the-meeting-madness (accessed May 2, 2019).

Schattner, E. August, 2012. "The Physician Burnout Epidemic: What It Means for Patients and Reform." *Health*. https://www.theatlantic.com/health/archive/2012/08/the-physician-burnout-epidemic-what-it-means-for-patients-and-reform/261418 (accessed January 21, 2019).

CHAPTER 8

Communication: Delivering Influential Messages

In the 2016 Athena Health *Physician Engagement and Leadership Index* of over 2,000 physicians, leadership traits most valued by physicians were identified with regard to their organizations' vision, culture, and day-to-day operations. It is notable that physicians overwhelmingly cited the ability to communicate as the most important skill for health care management! It was also the top leadership skill that physicians cited as the area of improvement that would most benefit the organization. When it was asked why physicians gave their leaders poor scores, the most common response was poor communication (Cosinuke 2015).

This finding is by no means a huge surprise. In our work with numerous organizations across industries, communication is the issue that surfaces the most with regard to leadership improvement. In his research, Joseph A. Klein, an Air Force psychologist and expert in leadership, has concluded that *if you can't communicate, don't lead* (Klein 2017).

We are always reluctant to present the basic, but necessary, guidelines for effective communication because we read and hear about them so often that it seems insulting to review them again. The subject of communication skills is well known to most of us. In fact, a search for communication books in Amazon turns up 80,000 results! We do not want to offend you with what may seem to be obvious. However, given that communication issues continue to surface most frequently as a significant problem in companies and organizations, we will provide an overview of what constitutes effective communication. After all, repetition is a required method for reinforcing what we know, and it does lead to a higher likelihood of utilization and implementation.

The primary purpose of any communication is to impact your audience in such a way that they will want to follow and follow through. Communication is a powerful way of creating understanding, connecting, and inspiring. According to communication studies, managers spend 70 to 90 percent of their time communicating with their team and others in the workplace. People at work will communicate more with each other than with their friends and family. Creating a culture that encourages successful communication increases the likelihood of having a productive staff. Effective communication gives a significant advantage to any leader. The goals of effective communication include the following (Luthra and Dahiya 2015):

- Fostering understanding
- Developing trust
- Creating positive relationships
- Creating a positive work environment
- Motivating employees
- Coordinating teams
- Building cohesiveness

We will look at the elements of effective communication that are fundamental to achieving these goals.

Effective Communication: Content and Process

Given these goals, it is clear that communication is more than a just a transfer of information. Effective communication for the physician-leader is the foundation for developing deep and meaningful relationships for the purpose of achieving far more together than could be achieved singularly. When employees complain about their managers or organizations not communicating effectively, their complaints are typically about the *volume* of unrelated communications they receive, the *consistency* of the messages they receive, the *frequency* with which they are included in receiving information that impacts their work, and the *manner* in which they receive the information, relative to its importance.

Communication always has two complementary aspects: content and process. Content is the more obvious element; it is what is written or said. Process has to do with the delivery of the message, including both the means and the intent. Research in the 1960s at the Mental Research Institute first identified that *how* a message is sent is as important as the content of the message. It was then that things like body language and the emotion with which messages are expressed were seen as having the ability to either reinforce the content of messages or contradict them. For example, saying "I am not angry!" with a scowl on your face and in a hostile manner certainly calls the content into question. We will discuss both aspects as a reinforcement for your own communication.

With regard to *content*, there are guidelines that can serve as a checklist for physician-leaders. In communicating it is always critical that messages have:

- Purpose: This answers the question "why am I interrupting your day?" When communicating to your target group, consider whether or not the communication reaches the threshold of warranting the time and attention it will be given. High levels of productivity are directly related to working on the most important issues. Diverting your team with unnecessary communication leads to reduced productivity and increased frustration.
- Precision and focus: Particularly when trying to communicate simple information, keep messages short and to the point without excessive verbiage. In this age of ever-changing technology, attention spans are increasingly shortened. People are used to slick, well-produced 30-second advertisements, and even small children know instantly what is meant by a familiar logo like the McDonald's golden arches. By providing headlines rather than the entire story, communications are much more likely to be read and understood. Invite your audience to ask for more information if they need it. When delivering complex information or tackling a difficult conversation (disciplinary or contentious), focus is key. Although conveying complex information may require a greater volume of communication, the skilled leader will take the time to pare down the message to just the essentials. Difficult conversations will sometimes require sacrificing brevity for the sake of navigating conflict or emotion. That said, approach the topic of the difficult

conversation directly without straying on tangents or introducing too much small talk.

- Transparency: Deliver communication that is clear with regard to intent, purpose, and expectations. This will help in increasing trust and loyalty. People are often suspicious that their superiors have some information that is not confidential but that they are not sharing with the rest of the employees. This veil of secrecy decreases trust and robs productivity by increasing speculation and gossip. When there is a lack of transparency, it implies that the managers do not trust the judgment of their team to use the information appropriately.

- Consistency: Messages to the team should be consistent over time. This is particularly true of large initiatives. Large organizations are notorious for following "the next big thing" only to abandon it before adequate momentum has developed. This start–stop tendency creates discouragement, cynicism, and lack of trust in management.

With regard to *process* too, there are key elements to be kept as high priorities. These include the following:

- Targets: Include only the people that will be impacted by the message, not everyone. This is not about CYA. E-mails and other communications that have a broad distribution list of people not impacted by the communication are a great time waster. When others are copied on communication, it creates the feeling that the communication is not personal, the sender is not discerning, and that there are hidden intentions for copying those for whom the message has little meaning. Leaders need to be diligent in regard to whom they are sending their communications and to send them only to those who need to know.

- Frequency: Keep targeted recipients informed without too many or too few communications. Always communicate when the message impacts the individual or when a response is required. When in doubt, err on the side of too many, not too few. Complaints are rarely that my manager communicated with me too often. Employees are much more likely to complain that they did not receive communication in a timely manner that allowed for adequate preparation.

- Attitude: All messages need to be respectful and gracious. Electronic messages (e-mails, texts, tweets, etc.), in particular, are not the right venue for airing differences, chastising, judging, or rebuking. These kinds of communications are always done privately and in person (see further on). Communications that consistently demonstrate respect and honor the involvement and time of the recipient always reap long-term rewards.
- Methodology: The method of communication delivery depends on how critical and complex the communication is. Below are the guidelines we recommend:
  - Personal: Any communication that is of a personal nature, particularly with either confidential or disciplinary messages, must always be conducted face-to-face. Although this seems obvious, when leaders are not effectively managing their emotions, they often violate this guideline and embarrass or humiliate the recipient.
  - Complex information: Information that is either complex or critical should be delivered face-to-face. This kind of communication often requires the kind of interaction for which personal involvement is required. It is an incredible waste of time and effort to try and solve difficult, complex issues electronically!
  - Confidential: There are often times when the leader has information that is very sensitive and can be shared only with a select number of people. As a general rule, this information should be shared face-to-face. Never e-mail or text confidential information unless you have electronic security.
  - Simple information: Information that is simple and direct does not need to be conveyed face-to-face and can easily be sent by text or e-mail (e.g. scheduling, agendas). Be sure to include only the audience that will be impacted.

These reminders will serve to help you become a more intentional communicator and will serve to increase both impact and productivity in the organization. Communication is as much a matter of effective delivery as it is precision in content.

Difficult Conversations: I'd Rather Not!

A subcategory of effective communication is that of managing difficult conversations. In our work with leaders across organizations, without exception the most dreaded interactions are those that involve some kind of conflict or disagreement. As a result, these conversations are often avoided or managed poorly. The reluctance to engage in these types of conversations stems from the expectation that they will be unpleasant, create discomfort, and lead to emotional distancing between the parties. The perception is often that the situation being set up is a zero-sum game, that is, where there will be a winner and a loser. In our experience with leaders needing to have difficult conversations, we often encounter three dysfunctional types of communicators. Each one of them seeks change but is ineffective because of insecurity, uncertainty, lack of clarity, and lack of confidence.

The Avoidant Communicator

These leaders dislike conflict and difficult conversations so much that they do not have them. They live by the rationalization of "let sleeping dogs lie." They justify their avoidance with the false belief that if you actually confront a situation it could become worse. They also hope that somehow things will get better on their own. Really? Often, you will know these leaders are unhappy only by their nonverbal behaviors like facial expressions or avoidance of certain people. It is a passive-aggressive way to demonstrate their displeasure. These leaders lose the respect of those they manage as they realize just how easy it is to take advantage of them because there are really no consequences!

The Under Communicator

These leaders recognize that a conversation needs to take place, but their discomfort leads them to provide only the scantiest details of their concerns. They can be blunt and overly direct, believing that their forcefulness will bring about the desired change. They may also be vague and nonspecific. In either case, these are sniper communicators who "pop in, pop off, and pop out," leaving the recipient confused and often resentful. You may feel dressed down with no recourse to respond or discuss the issue in any depth. These communicators succeed only at transferring their anxiety onto others!

The Circuitous Communicator

These leaders also recognize the need to have difficult conversations, but their discomfort leads them to take the long route. When approaching difficult conversations, these leaders spend excessive time talking about everything else such as your family, last week's ball game, the latest movie they saw, and anything but the topic of discord. Their communication is opaque and requires great powers of interpretation to understand the real reason for the meeting. Their "tell" is that they are having a lengthy conversation with you about innocuous content without ever getting to the point. Recipients of such communications begin to understand that their manager is upset but do not know about what. Worse yet, these circuitous communicators will let others know of their displeasure with you, but not tell you directly. You may learn about their displeasure only from the organization's grapevine. This is another passive-aggressive approach to dealing with conflict.

Managing Difficult Conversations

Leaders with high levels of emotional intelligence recognize that people are usually trying their best at any particular time. They do not shy away from having meetings when performance problems exist, and they recognize that they must be managed. These leaders enter difficult conversations with positive intent. They hold the belief that people want to be successful and recognize that when they are not, it is an opportunity for problem-solving, greater mutual understanding, and creating solutions that will be beneficial to the individuals and the organization. The desired outcome is not domination or win/lose. When entering conversations within this mental framework, it changes the situation from one that is fraught with pressure and antagonism to one in which both parties can become partners in creating solutions. The framework for these conversations is a multistep process that includes:

- Purpose: The leader must have a clear purpose in mind for the meeting. Clarifying what needs to be addressed and what is to be achieved are critical foundations to having a positive meeting. If the purpose is unclear, the leader should not proceed with the meeting.

- Preparation: These are not conversations where the leader can "shoot from the hip." These meetings are too important for haphazard planning. The leader needs to fully understand the issue(s) to be discussed and have an idea about what some acceptable outcomes may be. These meetings need to focus on the issue, not the person. The less emotion involved, the more effective the meeting can be. Managing emotions requires the leader to think about how to best bring up the issue and how to best respond. This is where leaders must have an attitude of positive intent and a belief that people want to learn and succeed. They trust that when people are not succeeding, creating the best environment or learning the right skills will prepare them for success.

- Presentation: These meetings are more formal and not "watercooler" chats. It is the leader's responsibility to lay out the issue in as much detail as is necessary to understand it. In presenting the issue, the leader must focus on the expectations, the results, and the gap between the two. Developing an understanding of root causes is central to creating viable solutions. The tone is not one of accusation or judgment but one of greater mutual understanding. The leader invites conversation to understand what may have led to the problem and what can be done to achieve the initial goals. The leader guides the conversation in such a way that both parties produce a mutually desired outcome, complete with clear expectations on quality, quantity, and timelines. In addition, they reach an understanding of what additional resources, if any, will be required to achieve the outcome agreed upon. The leader documents the conversation and shares a summary of the documentation with the employee.

- Follow-up: Initiatives often fail because a solid follow-up process has not been created or followed. Follow-up is a means of accountability and is critical for success. In order for the expectations and outcomes to be successful, the leader and the employee must have a process in place for follow-up. The leader will need to establish a schedule for "checking-in" and for monitoring progress as well as an understanding of when the issue discussed will be resolved.

By creating the above framework and following these steps, the dysfunctions associated with having difficult conversations can be avoided, or at least mitigated. Leaders need to keep in mind the principle of positive intent and remember that the goal of these conversations is greater mutual understanding and problem-solving for better results.

Special Exceptions

Although we advocate giving employees a second chance and positive thinking, we also recognize that when themes emerge they need to be treated differently than one-time events. There are two exceptions to the framework as outlined. In both cases, action is required.

1. Repetition Compulsion: We believe that the past is a prologue to the future. It has been our experience that when the process noted above has failed, repeating the process a second time will not usually yield different results. Unless there are unforeseen, and observable, obstacles or challenges, the employee's inability to effectively stick to the plan agreed upon is more closely related to either skill or will. If the employee is "in over his/her head," it may mean that a different position for the employee may be the answer. It could also mean that the employee needs further development or education to be successful. On the other hand, if it is a matter of lack of effort, it is unlikely that the employee will succeed in another position, and the leader needs to make a difficult choice in regard to the individual's employability.

2. Cause: When an employee has violated an ethical, moral, legal, or regulatory statute, the leader must manage the issue differently than noted previously. Any issue related to these violations carries a more serious weight than more routine performance-related problems. In all cases, the conversations must be factual, direct, and to the point. These violations typically entail more severe consequences that can range from personal improvement plans to suspensions or terminations. In all cases, clear documentation is required, and the human resources function is involved.

Case Study

Holding the Line While Maintaining the Relationship

The chairwoman of the board of directors of a rural hospital contacted us to help work with their CEO. Their CEO had previously been the chief medical officer (CMO). He had been with the hospital for several years. When the previous CEO retired, the CMO offered to step in on an interim basis while a search ensued. The board had not considered him for the position, at first, simply because they did not know of his interest. However, once they learned of his interest and, because he had been successful in the CMO position, the board convened an executive session, and the search committee of the board recommended the CMO for the CEO position without considering any other candidates. The board considered the savings in the cost of not hiring a search firm as well as the fact that he was available immediately and already knew the culture as significant factors in voting unanimously to accept the search committee's recommendation. It meant an almost seamless transition with virtually no time lost in the CEO's role.

Unfortunately, cracks began to appear 3 months following his appointment to the CEO role. The board chairwoman began to hear complaints about commitments not being met, conflicts escalating between department heads, and an increase in the level of negative rumors and innuendo. This was shocking to her because no such issues emerged when he was the CMO. In doing further research, she determined that the physician group was relatively self-managed when he was in the CMO position. The department chairs of all the major specialties were experienced, effective leaders who worked well with each other. Therefore, no significant problems had surfaced during his tenure as CMO. She and the board were very interested in the success of their new CEO, both for the success of the hospital and the message it sent to the rest of the organization if he failed. Because we had worked with the hospital previously, she contacted us to help.

We met with the CEO and the board chairwoman to develop a plan. We recommended one, and it was accepted. The plan was to engage the CEO in a 360-degree feedback process to pinpoint the issues and help create a development plan, followed by regular coaching sessions. We administered the 360-degree survey tool to the CEO, his subordinates, and the board chairwoman.

The results confirmed what we had suspected: the new CEO was having difficulty holding people accountable, both for their assignments and for their behaviors. On the 360-degree instrument, two specific items were identified, in which the CEO was not highly effective. He was not being *direct* with others when he was dissatisfied with their work, and he was failing to hold people *accountable*, not being firm when they did not deliver. These characteristics of being direct and holding others accountable have been found to be key traits for successful bosses. Research has determined that these two practices are the core requirements of creating organizational accountability (Kaiser 2019).

We reviewed the results with the CEO. These came as a surprise to him since they were not behaviors he was required to demonstrate in his previous CMO position. Nonetheless, he had a strong desire to succeed and work with us to create a development plan focusing on two critical goals. First, *setting clear expectations* that included the level of quality and production expected along with timelines. Second, *holding people accountable* for their performance when timelines or quality of tasks did not meet expectations. Both of these tasks require managing difficult conversations effectively. We further explained that, in a culture of accountability, great people thrive, whereas poor performers are exposed and often leave. Just the opposite happens when there is no accountability: competent people leave, while mostly poor performers remain. Neither setting clear expectations nor holding people accountable were part of the CEO's repertoire of behaviors. However, he understood that he needed to improve in both behaviors to be successful. We worked with the CEO over the next 6 months, coaching him on how to be more direct, set clear expectations, and hold others accountable. As of this writing, the CEO has successfully remained in his position for 5 years, having made the transition to a physician-leader that recognizes the critical importance of accountability in management.

The Physician-Leader Challenge

Physician-leaders face unique challenges when it comes to difficult conversations. For physician-leaders, many of their difficult conversations involve other physicians and often relate to disruptive, unprofessional behavior. How should a physician-leader approach these difficult conversations as both colleague and superior, clinician and administrator? In our experience, the strategy developed by Dr. Gerald Hickson and his colleagues at Vanderbilt is among the most effective for these difficult conversations (Hickson et al. 2007).

Dr. Hickson's model is a progressive approach that begins with an informal "cup of coffee" conversation. This is generally employed for seemingly new or isolated incidents. An important component of this intervention is to convey how much the physician is valued by the organization and how their current behavior is inconsistent with both organizational goals and the physician's reputation. The purpose of this informal conversation is to introduce awareness and early intervention with the hope of preventing a pattern of disruptive behavior.

When a pattern of disruptive behavior emerges, the next step is a more formal "Awareness" conversation, where data and information on the pattern is presented. If the behavior persists, an "Authority" intervention where repercussions are discussed occurs before the final step, the "Disciplinary" intervention occurs. For physician-leaders, it is important to understand and communicate which "hat" you are wearing during each conversation. The informal "cup of coffee" conversation is often conducted colleague to colleague, whereas the more formal conversations are typically superior to subordinate. Communicating which "hat" they are wearing allows physician-leaders to more clearly frame each conversation and its implications.

Coach's Corner

Despite being recognized for its importance, communication is the most common failure mode of leaders. Embracing the basics of effective communication will lay the groundwork for good leadership. Mastering the skills to successfully conduct difficult conversations is the foundation of great leadership.

1. **Identify your communication style**
   - Reflect on your natural inclination and current communication style as it relates to content and process discussed in this chapter. Is your communication style as effective as your organization needs? If not, what alterations to your communication style will make you more effective?

2. **Develop/refine your approach to difficult conversations**
   - Consider your approach to difficult conversations. Do you have any traits identified in the dysfunctional types of communicators? (Most leaders do!) Identify three specific tactics that you will work on to improve your skills in embracing or executing difficult conversations.

References

Cosinuke, R. July, 2015. "Communication Is the Most Important Leadership Trait." *athenainsight.* https://www.athenahealth.com/insight/communication-is-the-most-important-healthcare-leadership-trait (accessed February 1, 2019).

Hickson, G.B., J.W. Pichert, L.E. Webb, and S.G. Gabbe. November, 2007. "A Complementary Approach to Promoting Professionalism: Identifying, Measuring, and Addressing Unprofessional Behaviors." *Academic Medicine* 82, no. 11, pp. 1040–1048.

Kaiser, R. 2019. "The Accountability Crisis." *Talent Quarterly* 5, no. 3, pp. 57–63.

Klein, J. July, 2017. "Leadership and Communication." *APA Member Services.* https://www.apa.org/members/content/secure/leadership-communication (accessed February 7, 2019).

Luthra, A., and R. Dahiya. July–Sept 2015. "Effective Leadership Is All about Communicating Effectively: Connecting Leadership and Communication." *International Journal of Management & Business Studies* 5, no. 3, pp. 43–48. https://www.mcgill.ca/engage/files/engage/effective_leadership_is_all_about_communicating_effectively_luthra_dahiya_2015.pdf (accessed February 2, 2019).

CHAPTER 9

Negotiation: Competition or Collaboration

A subset of difficult conversations is that of negotiation. In this capacity, we are looking at those discussions in which leaders are bargaining for results that are of benefit to their organizations. The process for negotiating is related to having difficult employee conversations, but the audience is different, as are the issues being discussed. Leaders are regularly faced with opportunities to negotiate. In any negotiation, both parties want outcomes that are in their self-interest or the interest of their organizations. It is because these self-interests clash that negotiation is required. If they did not clash, they would not be negotiating. Each party wants to get at least some of what they want without having to give up too much.

It could be said that negotiation is part of everyday life and that we are all negotiators, except that we do not always recognize it as such. It happens in families when parents negotiate children's bed or bath times. It happens when couples negotiate the issue of who is going to take the dog out on a cold day. It happens at work when we discuss our remuneration. We negotiate when we buy a car or a house. Negotiating issues with physician-leaders will be different, but the principles we have found to be effective are the same. There are any number of negotiation strategies (high/low; walk away; take-it or leave-it; unreciprocated offers; bogeys; etc.). We want to help you create the frame for any negotiations, within which you can use whatever strategies seem most appropriate. We have identified several foundational elements to any negotiating process.

Clarifying the goal: It is important to be clear on what your goal in the negotiation is. To this end, it is important to gather data to support your position and to understand opposing points of view. It is also important to understand the goal and position of your counterpart. In both cases, it is important to understand that the ultimate goal has self-interest at its root. Understanding the motivations of your counterpart's self-interest is a necessary precondition for having a problem-solving mindset, rather than an adversarial one. It is similarly important to know those issues on which you are willing to compromise.

Setting the frame: The mindset going into a negotiation sets the frame for negotiation. Commonly, negotiation is seen as a battle. When the frame is characterized as a battle, the approach of both parties is that you have something I want, for which I want to give you very little. This frame sets up a win/lose situation at the outset. This approach is adversarial in nature. Power and domination are the prevailing behaviors. Although these competitive circumstances will periodically occur, it is important to realize that there are multiple possible approaches to negotiation.

Work at the Levinson Institute has determined that there are four basic negotiation strategies they call "The Four C's":

- Concession: a nonprocess where one party merely acquiesces to all the demands of the other (Lose–Win). This approach would occur when there is such a perceived power differentiation that for the weaker side to proceed, the potential damage could be even worse to them.
- Compromise: a process whose emphasis is on preserving relationships but whose outcome leads to a suboptimal solution that gives neither party enough of what they want to be satisfied (Lose–Lose). In this scenario, both sides believe that the relationship could be at risk if they were to proceed and that maintaining the relationship is more important than either side gaining an advantage.
- Competition: a process leading to one party achieving a high outcome and the other a low outcome without sustaining the relationship (Win–Lose). This is basically the value-claiming approach, in which the opposing sides are determined to get the outcome beneficial to them regardless of the impact on their opponent.
- Collaboration: a process for achieving mutually satisfying, optimal agreements while simultaneously building trust (Win–Win). This strategy is a value-creating approach, in which the two sides look for opportunities for both to get their desired outcomes with

the possibility that there are some innovative solutions that neither side had considered prior to the negotiation process. In this case, both sides place a high value on the relationship while maintaining a similarly high value on the outcome (Parekh 2012).

Graphically, these four negotiation strategies can be seen in Figure 9.1. This model presents the intersection of the importance of the negotiation

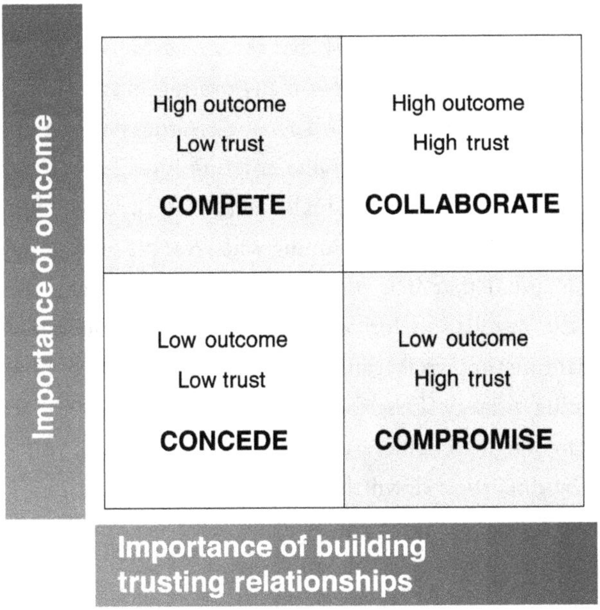

Figure 9.1 Negotiation scenarios and their strategies
Source: Parekh (2012).

outcome and the importance of the outcome to the two parties involved. As negotiations guru Chester Karrass has said, "In business, you do not get what you deserve, you get what you negotiate." This model is illustrative of that insight.

When going into any negotiation, it is important to consider the degree to which outcome is important and the degree to which relationship is important. With respect to outcome, conceding and compromising are value surrendering strategies. Although you may occasionally find yourself with no other options, only rarely should you be forced to resort to a value surrendering frame for negotiation. Competitive (value-claiming) and collaborative (value-creating) negotiations are much more common in the professional world. For that reason, we will be focusing the rest of this chapter on value-claiming and value-creating negotiation. Depending on the importance of the relationship, a value-creating negotiation is usually the preferred scenario, although a competitive, value-claiming negotiation is sometimes required or easier.

In short-term, transactional negotiations with strangers, the outcome is typically more important than the relationship. Think about the last time you bought a car. You know that the dealership was competing! In health care, as with most businesses, many relationships are long term and beneficial, predisposing you toward a value-creating negotiation strategy. When having a value-creating frame entering into the negotiation, the outcome is likely to be more mutually beneficial. Become diligent in focusing on the goal and not on winning whenever possible.

Keep in mind that it is possible, and often necessary, to shift the frame of the negotiation for other parties. Parties who initially adopt a value-claiming approach can sometimes be influenced to shift to a value-creating strategy. Describing the vision of a win–win scenario is sometimes enough to achieve this shift, but sometimes, you will need to drive the discussion down the path of value-creation, producing the initial understanding necessary to generate ideas that can demonstrate the potential of this approach to the other party.

Managing emotions: Even the most important decisions in life are made with a heavy dose of emotion. In fact, emotion often trumps reasoning and data. The same is true when negotiating. In an earlier chapter, we noted that effective leadership requires a high level of emotional intelligence. Nowhere is this skill more important than in a difficult negotiation. Having a clear understanding and control of your own emotional state is paramount for effective negotiating. When entering into negotiations with a win–lose mindset, the desire is to dominate rather than to understand. A win–lose mindset creates excessive emotion, anxiety, and anger, none of which benefit the negotiation process. Equally important is being observant of the emotional state of your counterpart so that you can both anticipate and appropriately respond to their queries or challenges. It is important to act rather than to react. In the most difficult times, demonstrating a calmness with a self-effacing sense of humor will offset tensions on both sides. It has been demonstrated that the inability to manage emotions leads to more errors in negotiations and significantly more financial loss than negotiations conducted in a neutral emotional state. Interestingly, these results exist regardless of whether the emotions are related to the negotiations or are incidental (Lerner 2005).

Creating a bond: Although the outcome of any negotiation is to have something that you did not have going into the process, negotiating is ultimately about relationships. Antagonistic relationships will result in antagonistic negotiations. We learn from hostage negotiators that bonding with those with whom we negotiate has the potential to have much better outcomes than not bonding. In addition, being willing to maintain a sense of humor is desirable, particularly one that is self-deprecating. You can be hard on issues but remain kind to people. Because negotiations are often serial in nature, you want to be remembered for the humane treatment you offered, rather than how difficult you were to deal with. Particularly in a value-creating negotiation, your counterpart needs to see you as a person who is approachable and not as an adversary.

Putting in the work to problem solve: If the frame you set is one of value-creating negotiation, the next step is to prepare yourself to put in the work necessary in taking a problem-solving approach. True collaboration keeps both parties' interests as the objects of focus, rather than their differences. Using this approach, all parties strive to arrive at a solution that best meets the underlying motivations of both parties. This means that the parties will commit the time necessary for deep conversations to better understand the reasons for their differences. Gaining a deep understanding of the other party and their motivations is the highest goal. Significant time needs to be spent on the front end of these talks to ensure that all parties have the same understanding of the problem or issue. This approach requires extensive exploration, using data, research, terms, and definitions about which both parties agree. The intent is to seek as much of a unified understanding of the issue as possible. This is the foundation of the ensuing brainstorming and genesis of ideas that is the basis of value-creation. There will always be compromises with the intent that small compromises for one party create substantial value for the other party. They keep in mind that they are not engaged in a "zero-sum" game.

"Agreeing to disagree" is not an acceptable response. This only shuts down productive discourse and ends negotiations. Rather, they are looking for creative options that will, as much as possible, satisfy the underlying interests of both parties. This is the hard work of a value-creating negotiation. In our experience, failure in these negotiations is usually the result of one or both parties not committing to do the heavy lifting required to produce success.

What to Do When All Else Fails

Rarely do negotiations go as expected. In fact, expecting the unexpected is a good mindset to maintain. Being fluid and creative is an antidote to being rigid and behaving defensively. Logic and reasoning will only go so far toward achieving the final result. Most negotiations are a dance where both parties have periods of yielding, compromising, and competing, even when negotiations are characterized by a problem-solving approach. Even with the best of intentions and utilizing all of the aforementioned skills, negotiations can stall. What do you do then?

BATNA: In any negotiation, an important concept to consider is the *best alternative to a negotiated agreement* (BATNA). Coined by Harvard Law School professors, Roger Fisher and William Ury (2011), this is a concept that will help you understand the context and leverage present in a negotiation. By definition, your BATNA is your best option if you fail to come to an agreement in the current negotiation. By knowing your BATNA, you can protect yourself from accepting terms that are too unfavorable and not in your best interest. On the other hand, if the proposed terms are better than your BATNA, you can either accept or continue to negotiate. Knowing both your and the other party's BATNA in a negotiation will give you a more accurate assessment of each party's leverage in the negotiation. It is always easier to assess your BATNA than it is to speculate about the other party's BATNA on the basis of whatever limited information you have. However, obtaining enough knowledge to have a good idea of the other party's BATNA can give you a significant advantage in the negotiation.

Understanding your own BATNA is also easier said than done. At first glance, your BATNA may seem obvious, but you need to make sure you have done your due diligence to consider all your possible alternatives.

One mistake that many leaders make is not calculating the comprehensive value of their alternatives. It may seem easy to compare the purely financial value of different alternatives, but, as always, the devil is in the detail. You must look beyond the apparent, basic revenue or costs and recognize the financial nuances that are hidden in the fine print. For example, one airline ticket may appear to be significantly cheaper than another until you consider additional costs such as add-on fees for baggage, specific seats, or refreshments.

Equally important, you must factor in nonfinancial factors such as operational constraints, levels of control and autonomy, commitment level required, and estimates of sustainability. Recognizing the high impact but nonfinancial components of each alternative and considering the associated value or cost to you will allow you to consider the comprehensive value of each alternative when determining your BATNA.

Ultimately, the BATNA is a construct that provides a simple framework on which to organize the knowledge you possess with regard to a particular negotiation. Depending on the subject of the negotiation, this knowledge may include clinical/operational expertise, evidence-based medicine, information about competitors, market trends, or the political environment. The more knowledge you possess in any negotiation, the more successful you will be. Can you imagine negotiating the purchase of a house without knowing the local market conditions, the interest rate environment, and the average sale price of comparable houses in the area? In any negotiation, it pays off to do your homework and research.

Case Study

Negotiating: Strength from Collaboration

A hospital system with which we consult was facing the upcoming renewal of its contract with a local health insurance company. The health insurance company had long contracted with the health system to be the sole provider of care to its insured patients in a narrow network model. These contracts were usually negotiated for renewal every 3 years. This year, the insurance company had decided that, rather than automatically renew the contract (typically with an incremental increase to cover inflation), they would create a Request for Proposal (RFP) and allow other local health systems to bid for the contract. In general, an RFP process is a value-claiming negotiation as opposed to a value-creating negotiation. Although they were not dissatisfied with the work of the health system with which they had been contracting, the insurer was always looking to manage costs while delivering quality care to its insured patients.

The CEO of the health system called us and asked for advice to navigate the RFP process. We recommended that the CEO take a proactive approach and meet with the insurance company prior to the release of the RFP. We encouraged the health system CEO to use this meeting to start a dialogue about the needs of both the insurance company and the health system. At a minimum, this in-depth discussion and exploration would provide the health system with valuable information to create an RFP response while also helping the insurance company consider its needs and desires.

The CEO did as we recommended and met with the insurance company not once but multiple times. During these meetings, the health system and the insurance company learned about the current state of their organizations' relationship with one another. They also learned more about opportunities and challenges of both organizations. Through many hours of discussion, the health system came to understand how to create a proposal that benefited both the health system and the insurance company. For its part, the insurance company was able to determine the nuances of exactly what it was looking for in a health system partner.

At the conclusion of the RFP process, the health system CEO was overjoyed to learn that they had won the contract to continue a narrow network partnership with the health insurance company. However, by taking the time to educate both his own organization and the insurance company, the health system CEO was able to turn a value-claiming negotiation into more of a value-creating negotiation. The new partnership that was forged between the two organizations had greater synergy and provided greater benefit for both organizations.

The Psychology of Negotiation

As powerful as knowledge can be in a negotiation, psychology also plays a significant role. One example of this involves the process of making the first offer. In our experience, there is a prevailing belief that you should never make the first offer in a negotiation. Popular opinion suggests that by doing so, you risk "showing your cards" too early, negatively impacting the negotiation. To the contrary, studies have shown that making the first offer has positive effects on the results of a negotiation. These studies suggest that making the first offer sets the tone and anchors the negotiation in favor of that party. This anchoring effect is primarily psychological, effectively influencing the thought process of the other party regardless of the knowledge and facts they carried into the negotiation. Interestingly, it has also been demonstrated that actively considering the other party's BATNA, and hence the least attractive deal they may be willing to accept, can eliminate the anchoring bias of the first offer. In other words, actively focusing on the facts after the first offer is made can counteract the psychological factors in play. This area of study confirms the strong effects of psychology in negotiation while reinforcing how essential it is to be informed and to also intentionally focus on that information.

In a previous chapter, we discussed the interaction of nature and nurture as being instrumental in differentiating the physician from the general population. Not surprisingly, both brain functioning and personality play a role in negotiation. In all human activity, there is brain involvement that influences and determines how we behave. The area of negotiation is no different. Neuroimaging studies have determined that several brain systems are involved in negotiations. Research at the Max Planck Institute for Human Cognitive and Brain Sciences in Germany used real-time *functional magnetic resonance imaging* (fMRI) to better understand neural correlates of social decision making. They found that the anterior insula, ventral striatum, and lateral orbitofrontal cortex appear to be strong determinants of later overt behavior in negotiation situations (Hollmann et al. 2011). The research was able to reliably predict acceptance or rejection of an offer in a negotiation *before* the subject revealed the decision with an overt response. This occurred with a 70 percent prediction rate.

Researchers found that the negotiation process can be broken down into three phases: preparation, the offer, and the response. Within each of these, the brain is processing significant amounts of information in a different part of the brain to help the negotiator guide the best outcome. They determined that during negotiation there are three phases and three brain systems (Hollmann et al. 2011). The reason these findings are important is that negotiation is typically seen as a rational process in which one party is trying to outwit the other through both strategic moves and behavioral cues. However, the research has demonstrated that in a competitive negotiation, the dopamine system is really driving behavior. Competition can bias the way the brain weighs rewards and can influence overpaying if the competition becomes fierce. So, when the autonomic nervous system goes into overdrive, triggering a quickened heart rate and sweating, the dopamine system is kicking in, and the negotiator is at risk for becoming overly aggressive.

There is also a relationship between negotiation and the Big Five Personality Factors. Research has determined that *agreeableness, conscientiousness,* and *extraversion* recur as the most statistically relevant factors in negotiation. The research focused on both traditional negotiation (value-claiming) and problem-solving negotiation (value-creating). The type of negotiation determines the degree to which these traits are effective (Falcão et al. 2018). The results indicated that *conscientiousness* played a significant role in both kinds of negotiation. This finding is likely due to the role of planning and being prepared prior to entering into a negotiation. There is no substitute for planning, and "shooting from the hip" weakens the negotiation process. It is important to differentiate between being impulsive and being creative.

Extraversion played a positively related role in both types of negotiation. In the problem-solving negotiation, *adaptable* extraversion was instrumental in coming to a positive outcome. This would be expected from the standpoint that adaptable extraversion would lead one to demonstrate a collaborative tone for problem solving. This is likely related to the degree to which adaptable extraverts can appear to be cooperative, gregarious, and social. In the problem-solving negotiation, parties recognize that competition may be counterproductive, so extraverts may need to temper their dominant tendencies.

However, in the traditional value-claiming negotiation, *extraversion* that included more dominant, competitive behaviors was instrumental in positive outcomes. Demonstrating competitive behaviors helps when one party seeks to get more than the other party. When there is either a zero-sum game or a win–lose outcome, a domination-oriented approach to negotiation can assist. In these negotiations, demonstrating a minimum concern for social relationships and maximizing assertiveness were instrumental in achieving the desired outcomes.

Agreeableness had mixed findings, being both a virtue and a curse. In competitive negotiation, agreeableness had a negative influence. By agreeing too quickly, and too often, it can imply that the party wishes to accept outcomes that are less rigorous than his or her counterpart. This can seem to be a weakness in negotiations characterized by competitive domination and puts the opponent in a superior position. In these negotiations, maintaining a low level of agreeableness, including offering fewer concessions, is advantageous. However, in problem-solving negotiations, a balanced level of *agreeableness* facilitates a desire to seek beneficial outcomes for both parties. It indicates that the parties want collaboration over competition. When using problem-solving negotiations, being more agreeable reduces defensiveness and dominant behavior, and it is foundational to positive interactions. At the same time, the negotiator must have a balanced level of agreeableness, as excessive *agreeableness* can result in conceding rather than seeking mutually beneficial outcomes. A summary of the personality traits required for successful negotiation in both value-creating and value-claiming negotiations is found in Figure 9.2.

Personality traits	Value-claiming negotiation	Value-claiming negotiation
Conscientiousness	High conscientiousness (preparation)	High conscientiousness (preparation)
Extraversion	Adaptable extraversion	Dominant extraversion
Agreeableness	Balanced agreeableness	Low agreeableness

Figure 9.2 Desired personality traits and successful negotiation strategies

Source: Falcão et al. (2018).

Psychology of Negotiation for Physician-Leaders

As you will recall from Chapter 3, the typical physician is high in *conscientiousness, extraversion, and agreeableness,* but does vary by specialty and individual physician. Knowing your personality construct before entering into negotiations is clearly important. In particular, understanding the tendencies to which you are *conscientious, extraverted,* and *agreeable* are prerequisites for managing these traits. Once you understand these tendencies, tailoring your behavior to the negotiation situation will assist in coming to the desired outcome.

In health care settings at an organizational level, a problem-solving, value-creating approach is typically desired more than one that is competitive and value claiming. In value-creating negotiation, collaboration is valued more than competitiveness. Positive interpersonal relationships are valued, in which parties are seeking solutions that benefit the greater good. This implies that all parties are "on the same team" and seeking mutually desirable outcomes. When physician-leaders find themselves in negotiation situations, they need to help set the frame early so that they can determine the kind of negotiation they are facing and adapt their styles accordingly.

Coach's Corner

Negotiation is an omnipresent component of both professional and personal life. As such, it can feel second nature and almost simplistic. Yet effective negotiation is both a science and an art. With thorough preparation and proper strategy, physician-leaders can reap the rewards of fruitful negotiation.

1. **Identify your natural tendencies in regard to negotiation**
   - Using your personal psychological profile that you identified in Chapter 3, reflect on how your natural tendencies will influence you in a negotiation. Understanding your natural inclinations, what approach and tactics should you employ to be most effective in a negotiation? How should you play on your strengths and mitigate your weaknesses?

2. **Always identify your BATNA**
   - In every negotiation, take time to identify your realistic Best Alternative to a Nonagreement. It is easy to fall into the trap of letting assumptions or emotion guide a negotiation instead of starting with facts such as your BATNA.

3. **Practice makes perfect**
   - Recognize and embrace all of your opportunities to negotiate both in your personal and professional life. You will find that they occur almost daily. Practice applying the personal tactics you have identified, and assess your success in each instance.

References

Falcão, P.F., M. Saraiva, E. Santos, and M.P. Cunha. June, 2018. "Big Five Personality Traits in Simulated Negotiation Settings." *EuroMed Journal of Business* 13, no. 2, pp.201–213. https://www.emeraldinsight.com/doi/abs/10.1108/EMJB-11-2017-0043?journalCode=emjb (accessed February 7, 2019).

Fisher, R., and W. Ury. 2011. *Getting to Yes: Negotiating Agreement without Giving in.* 3rd ed. New York, NY: Penguin Books.

Hollmann, M., J.W. Rieger, S. Baecke, R. Lützkendorf, C. Müller, D. Adolf, and J. Bernarding. October, 2011. "Predicting Decisions in Human Social Interactions Using Real-Time fMRI and Pattern Classification." *PLoS One* 6, no. 10, p. e25304. https://doi.org/10.1371/journal.pone.0025304 (accessed February 7, 2019).

Lerner, J.S. 2005. "Negotiating under the Influence: Emotional Hangovers Distort Your Judgment and Lead to Bad Decisions." *Negotiation* 8, no. 6, pp. 1–3. https://projects.iq.harvard.edu/lernerlab/publications/negotiating-under-influence-emotional-hangovers-distort-your-judgment-and-lea (accessed March 6, 2019).

Parekh, R. 2012. *Collaborative Negotiation.* Jaffrey, NH: The Levinson Institute, Inc.

SECTION 3

Physician-Leadership: A Culmination

CHAPTER 10

The Physician-Leader's Pocket Guide

The transition from clinician to physician-leader is one that requires adaptability, curiosity, perseverance, patience, and open-mindedness. Most of all, it requires the ability of the physician to be versatile. Being versatile means having a willingness to change behavior and adapt to the situation or role of leadership. As you have read in previous chapters, the very characteristics that make for being an outstanding physician can be the same behaviors that undermine the work in leadership roles. In fact, having an unwillingness to adapt ensures that the clinician will fail at becoming an effective leader. As coaching guru Marshall Goldsmith has observed, "What got you here will not get you there" (Goldsmith 2007). In his book, Goldsmith takes the reader through the reasons why moving up in any organization requires different skills and behaviors than previous positions required. Nowhere is this more evident than with the physician who is moving into a leadership position.

Research on leadership has determined that the most effective leaders are those that demonstrate the ability to adapt their styles to the circumstances with which they are faced. In fact, the correlation between leadership effectiveness and versatility is 0.71 when looking at both how a leader leads and on what the leader is focused (Kaplan and Kaiser 2008). Versatile leaders are able to moderate their leadership behavior to fit the situation with which they are faced. What leaders focus on, tactics or strategy, is only half the story. The other half, and arguably the most important half, is *how* leaders lead, ranging from being empowering on one end to being forceful on the other. It is how the leader leads that will ultimately determine the degree of influence and followership he or she has achieved.

What we have attempted to show you in this book are the foundational skills physicians need to learn and the behaviors they need to adopt in order to become effective physician-leaders. We will review here the central characteristics required for that transition.

Understanding the Role

The transition from being a full-time clinician to having a leadership role, even part time, is a complex and challenging move. It is a move that requires learning new skills and changing some behaviors. We have reiterated that the capabilities and skills that make good physicians are often at odds with those that make good leaders. Our tendency as humans is always to default to those behaviors with which we are most comfortable. This is particularly true in times of stress or pressure. The ability to resist using old behaviors and risk using new ones is always a bit scary. Know that you will initially proceed by fits and starts as you try on some of the new behaviors necessary for effective leadership. They will become easier with repetition, practice, and success.

One of the primary changes from being a clinician to being a physician-leader is moving into a role of managing, rather than directing. This means that the physician will become more of an influencer than the authority. It means harnessing the wide expanse of skills and intellect in others. Using collaboration and negotiation are the centerpieces of effective leadership. This requires patience, taking a longer view, and thinking more strategically than is required in the purely clinical role. The physician-leader also needs to transition from the clinical hub-and-spoke leadership style to one in which leadership is shared, capitalizing on the strengths of individuals on the team.

The Business of Health Care

In the changing world of health care, the health care model is changing from one that is professional-centered and focused on effectiveness and volume to one that is patient-centered and focused on value. The business model for health care is still unsettled, but we know it is going to change and likely to do so rapidly. The physician-leader will need to understand what this means in terms of services, patients, physicians, vendors, insurers, pharmaceutical companies, and so on. When the focus is on creating value, rather than primarily on increasing volume, the physician-leader will have to know the many ways required to deal with this paradigm shift.

The leader will also need to understand what value discipline the hospital or health care organization will be working toward maximizing. Health care organizations will be required to excel at operational efficiency, product and service innovation, or customer intimacy. They will need to be outstanding in at least one of these aspects and average or above in the other two, in order to survive. Understanding how these value disciplines fit into the new health care business model will be a challenge every physician-leader will be facing. The physician-leader will also need to understand and be conversant in the metrics of health care. Understanding that it is metrics that serve as the scoreboard and help to identify system strengths and weaknesses will help the physician-leader know where to direct resources for maximum benefit.

The Personality of the Physician

Physicians have unique personalities, shaped by both genetics and the environment in which they developed. These unique personality traits are further shaped by the specialty that the physician has chosen. The demands of being a clinician and the responsibility of managing and overseeing the health of their patients typically create individuals who are more *conscientious* than the average professional. They also tend to demonstrate more *agreeableness* and more *extraversion* than the average professional. These traits vary some according to specialty, but are all higher than the population as a whole.

It is these very traits that have made physicians such good clinicians. They possess the ability to engage with their patients, understand their symptoms, and prescribe the best treatment. In this role, they are the authority and make decisions independently. Although some of these traits translate well into leadership positions, some can be handicaps. In particular, the penchant toward perfectionism and the tendency to make decisions independently both have to be modified when moving into a leadership position. We recommend that clinicians considering the move into leadership positions assess their personalities to better understand what traits they will want to begin working on as they transition into a leadership role.

Qualities of an Effective Leader

Leadership is about influence. Without influence, no one will follow and nothing will get done. The good news is that the characteristics of an effective leader have been identified so that aspiring leaders can better learn the behaviors they will need to have to be most effective. We have created a formula for influence.

Influence = CARVE

The components of this formula are:

Courage: the willingness to stand up for what is right in the face of opposition.

Authenticity: having behaviors that are congruent with your expressed beliefs and values, that demonstrate a high degree of humility, and that are accompanied with personal vulnerability.

Rational Appeal: using intellectual reason, appealing to the rational side of those with whom you interact.

Values: having a core set of values that guide your behavior and are congruent with the values of your constituents.

Emotional Intelligence: understanding and managing your emotions and the emotions of others.

It is our experience that the best leaders have all of these qualities and use them on a regular basis to engage their teams. By regularly and consistently using these components, you will be able to turn these new behaviors into internalized traits. In other words, they become a part of you. Although being a strong leader and influencer is not easy, the quest is worth the effort. Talent is in high demand, but the shortage of good leaders is alarming.

Setting a Vision

In order to have an engaged workforce, it is important for those in the organization to believe that they are involved in meaningful work and that their work is tied to something greater than themselves. The most effective leaders understand this and know the importance of having a mission, vision, and strategies that are all aligned and consistent with the organization's goals.

Effective leaders also know that organizations can only withstand so much change at a time. In fact, the more goals an organization has, the less likely it will be to accomplish any of them. The most successful organizations have no more than three to five major goals, all of which align with the organization's vision and have metrics to track them. Creating a successful vision is the starting point for any organization to succeed. It provides the compass, road map, steering wheel, and engine to get to the final destination most efficiently.

Building a High-Performing Team

Nothing gets done without people. Nothing gets done well without a high-performing team. There are two areas in which teams must excel in order to be considered high performing, and those areas are *productivity* and *vitality*. Productivity may seem obvious. It is the total output of any team in terms of the products and services that it is creating or providing for customers. It would be expected that high performance goes hand in hand with high productivity. But there is a second, equally compelling characteristic that must be met, and that is *how* the productivity is attained. Vitality requires high morale, interpersonal cohesion and employee engagement, which are all necessary for the team to be considered high performing.

Productivity and vitality are both *outcomes* of having all of the elements of a high-performing team in place. A team needs to have the right people with the right skills; a clear charter with a clear focus; a strong climate that is safe and allows for differences of opinion and points of view; a process for effective execution, including collaboration, accountability, and incentives; and clear communication, including processes to resolve conflict. It is the responsibility of an effective leader to put all of these into place in order for the team to maximize its potential.

Magnifying Impact through Delegation

One of the biggest challenges of the physician-leader is that of delegation. There is always more work to do than any one person can accomplish. However, because physicians are so high in *conscientiousness*, they tend to be perfectionists and have difficulty trusting others to get work done appropriately. As a result, it is not uncommon for the physician-leader to either take on too much themselves or, when they do delegate, micromanage the work.

Learning how to delegate is more complicated than it would first appear. It is more than simply allotting work to others. The most effective delegators have a process in place that includes differentiating between what work can be delegated; what work is not worthy of being done now or maybe at all; and what work leaders must do themselves. Once they have differentiated, they have a clear strategy about whom to delegate to, rather than delegating randomly. Finally, they have a process of follow-up to ensure that work they have delegated will get done properly. Leaders need to think of delegating as a way to magnify their impact in the organization and not simply as a way to get work completed.

Communicating to Make a Difference

The ability to communicate effectively is the most important skill for health care management. This is not surprising since it is the most widely cited complaint employees have in most organizations. The most effective physician-leaders are aware of the need to keep their teams informed and understand that it is not only the content of their messages but also the *way* in which information is conveyed that is important. These leaders are consistently working to ensure that everyone has the information they need to get their jobs done effectively.

Dealing effectively with conflict is a type of communication that even good leaders tend to avoid or delay. Having difficult conversations is anathema to those physician-leaders high in *agreeableness*. These leaders just want everyone to get along! However, conflict in the workplace is inevitable. The smart leader is one that understands this and further understands that delaying or postponing difficult conversations will only exacerbate them in the future. Creating a process for having difficult conversations that are problem-solving in nature, rather than blaming or judging, is a necessary step for holding people accountable and ensuring fair treatment for all. The best leaders attack conflict head-on and with the expectation that the outcome will be the best for all parties involved.

Successful Negotiating Strategies

Surveys have found negotiation to be one of the top skills that physicians want to learn and master. It is no wonder because negotiation is a constant in a physician's life from negotiating schedules to negotiating contracts. Too often, negotiations are entered into with a zero-sum game approach in which participants are determined to gain something from their opponent and expect that their opponent will have to lose something of equal value. It is the height of competitiveness and, in negotiation terms, is a *value-claiming* approach to negotiations characterized by low trust and high competition.

A more productive negotiation style is a *value-creating* approach. This approach relies on collaboration and high levels of trust. The goal is to create an outcome that is beneficial to both parties, and the methodology is one of mutual problem-solving rather than one of high competition. This is the more desirable of the two strategies but requires both parties to take the risk of believing that each party has the other's best interest in mind. Regardless of your negotiation strategy, doing your homework to arm yourself with knowledge is the key to success.

Wellness in Physician-Leadership

Physician wellness has been a trendy and important topic in medicine for many years. There is little doubt that the pressures of being a physician and taking the ultimate responsibility for the health care of other humans are unique challenges that layer onto the typical frailties of the human race in a manner that has created an epidemic of physician burn-out. Physician-leader wellness, while related, has its own set of hurdles.

In the previous chapters of this book, we have outlined many of the common difficulties that physicians face as they transition into leadership. A few of these obstacles factor strongly into the wellness equation for physician-leaders.

As with any career path, it is important for the physician-leader to recognize the aspects of their role that bring them joy. This is why it is so crucial for physician-leaders to understand why they are drawn to leadership. It is easy for physicians to be pushed into leadership, because the need is so great. It is equally common for physicians to run toward leadership roles because they are suffering burnout in their clinical careers. The good news is that leadership is diverse in its responsibilities. If the physician-leader can identify what brings them passion and joy in work, they can usually figure out a way to infuse that into their roles. Whether they are driven by mentoring and developing others, creating strategy, driving clinical quality, or even reducing burnout in other physicians, the intentional physician-leader can energize their careers by feeding their passions. The key is recognition and intentionality.

Prioritization is also a requisite skill for the healthy physician-leader. In clinical medicine, the checklist is a force unto itself. The clinician must accomplish every single task on the checklist in order to ensure that their patients receive the proper care. In leadership, this virtue is a curse. Administrative and leadership duties are not prescribed in the way that clinical care can be, especially in this age of evidence-based medicine. The to-do list for leaders is literally never ending. Beyond merely prioritizing potential tasks, the physician-leader must learn to draw the line at a reasonable place and not only accept but also be comfortable leaving all the tasks below that line undone. This is true of both short- and long-term initiatives and can be greatly mitigated with effective delegation. Failure to master this skill will result in frustration, self-doubt, and eventually burnout.

Another peril that awaits the physician-leader involves the concept of delayed gratification and subtle rewards. Clinical medicine is rife with long hours, daily annoyances, and sad patient stories. However, physicians repeatedly report that it is the intermittent wins like making a good diagnosis or having a great patient outcome that keeps them going. In leadership, the wins are different and the time frames of initiatives protracted. As a result, physician-leaders can find a dearth of positive reinforcement in the short term. Even in the long term, it is easy to work on an initiative for many months only to successfully achieve the goal and move on to the next initiative, never stopping to recognize the accomplishment. The successful physician-leader will learn to recognize the small victories. These may be milestones along the way to accomplishing broader goals. Moreover, leaders must derive gratification from accomplishments such as having an engaged staff or a positive organizational culture. Physician-leaders will also need to understand that the work of leadership is measured over years, not days or weeks. It takes experience and faith to embrace this concept. Leadership can be very isolating, so developing a support structure of trusted colleagues can help to keep success in perspective.

Wellness is now an entire field of study, and concepts such as meditation, mindfulness, and practicing or journaling gratitude can certainly benefit the physician-leader. We believe that pairing the leadership-specific material contained in this section with other universal wellness techniques can help ensure that physician-leaders maintain healthy and fulfilling lives.

What You Need to Know about Being a Physician-Leader: FAQs

There are several questions that we have been asked that go beyond the scope of this book but are important to becoming a physician-leader. We try to answer the most popular ones here.

- **Do I need an MBA to be a successful physician-leader?**
  This is perhaps the most common question asked by aspiring physician-leaders. A Master of Business Administration (MBA) or similar degree is certainly useful to provide physician-leaders with the basic knowledge and skills for management. It is also a positive factor on the resume when applying for a leadership position. However, an MBA alone is like attending medical school without doing

a residency. The skills and experience gained in actual leadership roles are much more impactful in creating effective physician-leaders. So, while an MBA might help secure a first job in leadership, its benefit for an experienced physician-leader is somewhat muted. As with all great questions, there is no easy answer, and each physician-leader must answer this question for themselves. A student entering medical school with the idea of pursuing physician-leadership would be well served to consider one of many existing joint MD–MBA programs. An already practicing physician will likely have a more complex cost-benefit analysis.

There are a variety of other avenues available for physician-leaders to gain leadership education. The American Association of Physician-leadership offers regular conferences and a curriculum to become a Certified Physician Executive (CPE). Medical Group Management Association (MGMA) and the American College of Healthcare Executives (ACHE) also have educational offerings that can be useful for physician-leaders. Opportunities for physician-leader education grow every year, and a quick Internet search can reveal many options.

- **How can I move from the clinical work I do into a full-time leadership role?**
  Clinicians often ask us how they can move into leadership roles. Very few people apply to medical school with the intent to become a physician-leader. As such, the path to physician-leadership varies widely from one leader to the next. The commonality is that most begin their careers as clinicians and spend some time dabbling with various administrative roles before making the leap to being a full-time physician-leader. There are ample opportunities in any health care organization for physicians to serve in limited administrative roles. This is usually the first step for clinicians who want to become leaders. By volunteering for committees or workgroups, clinicians both express their interest in leadership and demonstrate to established organizational leaders that they have the foundational skills to be a leader. Examples of readily available committees are in the areas of quality, patient safety, peer review, credentialing, utilization review, and case management.

Physicians who can demonstrate the foundational skills described in this book are sure to be noticed as potential leaders. There is such a need for physician-leaders that one opportunity usually leads to another, larger opportunity. The committee member becomes the committee chair. The committee chair becomes the medical director, and so on.

This process usually takes years but can move much faster depending on the organizational needs. During this time, physicians should find and take advantage of chances to gain formal leadership education from courses or conferences. Often, organizations are willing to support this education with time and resources. Up and coming physician-leaders must eventually decide that they want to make the leap to a full-time leadership role and keep themselves abreast of such opportunities that develop at their institutions. It is usually easiest to transition into a full-time leadership role at your own organization as you are a known commodity. Once you have the experience and the title on your resume, the path to a leadership role at another organization is much easier.

- **What things do I need to learn to be an effective physician-leader?** The leadership skills discussed in this book are foundational and will translate effectively to any leadership role. There is also subject matter specific to health care and physician-leaders. Quality and patient safety are areas that all physician-leaders should understand. From basic quality improvement tactics such as a plan-do-study-act cycle to more advanced techniques such as six-sigma and lean management, physicians-leaders must possess at least the foundations of this knowledge. Once armed with this quality improvement skill set and a willingness to embrace change, a physician-leader's clinical training can make them uniquely qualified to contribute to clinical quality improvement efforts. The compliance and regulatory realm is another territory where physician-leaders need to be comfortable. Understanding Stark and Anti-kickback laws, The Emergency Medical Treatment and Labor Act (EMTALA), Joint Commission regulations, and a myriad of other health care regulations is crucial. Physician management often falls under the purview of a physician-leader, so knowledge of credentialing, privileging, peer review, and physician health/ rehabilitation is essential. A basic knowledge of finance and accounting becomes increasingly important as a physician-leader moves up in an organization. This includes the ability to understand budgeting, profit and loss statements, and pro formas. These represent some major areas of required expertise for physician-leaders, but there are many others. Each of these topics warrants a book of its own so we did not attempt to address them in this book. We encourage all physician-leaders to make these topics a part of their education.

- **Is there any value in engaging an outside coach to help me learn about leadership?**

  As we have discussed in detail, the skills that are required for becoming an excellent physician can sometimes interfere with the ability to become an effective leader. It has been our experience that engaging an executive coach to help you with this transition can be extremely helpful for developing new behaviors and insights for leadership. One underrecognized benefit of coaching for physician-leaders is the reassurance that a coach can provide. All leaders are prone to feeling alone and isolated. As the saying goes, it can be lonely at the top. New physician-leaders often go through a period of self-doubt and discomfort with their new role even if they are doing a great job. A coach can provide the reassurance needed to push on. A word of caution: do your due diligence. Because there are few regulations or standards for advertising oneself as a coach, there is a very wide variation in expertise and quality. It is important to have a coach that understands health care, business, leadership, and psychology. Comparing resumes and credentials could be helpful.

- **Would a personality assessment help me become a better leader?**

  Having greater self-understanding can be an asset to any position in which you find yourself. This is particularly true when making the transition from a clinician to a physician-leader. When used with ongoing coaching, personality assessments can help focus the coaching and lead to positive behavior change. Like coaches, there are a wide variety of individuals who provide this service as well as a wide variety of assessments available. Having an unqualified assessor with a poor instrument can be of little value. As we have stated in Chapter 3, assessments that look at the Big Five Personality Traits have become standard in the personality assessment field. In particular, the Hogan suite of assessments are what we recommend without reservation (hoganassessments.com). In addition, we have found the Leadership Versatility Index (LVI) to be an excellent 360-degree assessment (kaiserleadership.com). Although there are good assessments available, make sure that the assessments you use have high levels of reliability and validity and that they are administered by individuals with certification or licensure in your state.

Lessons along the Way: Leadership Pearls We Have Learned

In our over 50 years of combined experience in health care and learning about leadership, several pearls of wisdom have guided us, on which we rely to make decisions. These pearls have come from both the school of hard knocks and from sage mentors and teachers we have had. As a closing note on our book on leadership, we want to share these with you. You can use them like a reference card in the pocket of your white coat when you need help—Leadership Made Ridiculously Simple. We hope you will add these to your own lessons learned. It is our hope that these pearls become part of your ongoing education as you move into a physician-leader role.

- **Not everyone is like you:**
  All people have their own way of thinking and acting. Since your perspective and approach is the one most familiar to you, it is common to fall into the thinking that other people should think and act the way you do. This can create frustration for leaders as something that seems simple to the leader may be an enormous challenge for others. Change management is a core task of leadership, and it is so difficult precisely because people are all unique in their thinking. We have repeatedly coached frustrated leaders to remember this concept and seek unity in diversity, rather than discounting those who may think differently.

- **Understand the perception–reality gap, both yours and others':**
  Everyone has a perception of themselves and their own abilities. It is not uncommon for this perception to differ from that of others as well as from objective measures. We have found that the most effective people and leaders are able to recognize the gap between their perception and reality. Diminishing that gap between reality and perception is a necessary condition for self-awareness, maximal effectiveness, and authenticity. It has been said that the most dangerous doctor is the one that doesn't know what they don't know. This is a perception–reality gap.

- **Narrate your leadership as you would narrate your care:**
  In a leadership position, staff and subordinates are very much like your patients. They become anxious when they don't know what to expect, what you are going to do, and what their role is in your plan. The more you communicate both your plan and your expectations, the less the anxiety and the greater the buy-in and compliance you will get.

- **Be comfortable swimming in the gray:**
  The physician/patient role is one in which both parties want certainty. Patients want to know their diagnosis and treatment. Physicians want certainty with patient diagnosis and treatment. Human beings, in general, take comfort in certainty. However, in leadership roles, things are almost never black and white. In fact, there is typically significant ambiguity when solving systemwide problems, and there is often more than one solution. The tasks of leadership also commonly take time to come to resolution. Physician-leaders need to become comfortable with *not* knowing and with the process of patiently exploring rather than having definitive answers. This is easier said than done. The discomfort of uncertainty and swimming in the gray has been the downfall of many new leaders.

- **Success is in the process, not just the outcome:**
  As a leader, when solving large, complex, and unfamiliar problems, it is important to put in place the best processes and trust that the best answers will emerge. Being able to separate the outcome from the value of the leader is a difficult but important skill. The best leaders recognize that their responsibility is to address every

challenge in the best way possible as that will produce the highest likelihood of success. At the same time, the healthiest leaders are capable of accepting that negative outcomes sometimes occur despite their best efforts, as not everything is within their control.

- **Patience is your ally**:
  The great Russian author Leo Tolstoy observed that in life "[t]he two most powerful warriors are patience and time." Clinical practice requires that decisions be made on the spot and, sometimes, with very little time to consider multiple options. The opposite is true in leadership. Although there are threats and crises that require immediate attention, they are very infrequent. By far, these are the exception rather than the rule in leadership decision making. Effective leadership requires processes that include seeking input from multiple sources, weighing the benefits and risks of various scenarios, and looking for trends that indicate a theme. These processes require leaders to have patience and to be willing to take more time when making big decisions than is afforded the clinician. In leadership, time and patience are your allies.

- **Don't oversolve the problem**:
  The philosopher Voltaire observed that "the perfect is the enemy of the good." We have learned that physicians are typically highly *conscientious*, often to the point of being perfectionists. When working with patients, this trait is extremely helpful in making an accurate diagnosis and creating effective treatment plans. However, this same level of perfectionism in a leadership role can serve to bring progress to a halt because of the extraordinary time involved in getting to the "right" solution. The problems of systems often do not require a perfect solution, but only one that is "good enough." It is important not to overengineer solutions. Do not let your pursuit of perfection sabotage getting a good solution in place.

- **Leadership is a series of ups and downs, victories and losses, problems and solutions**:
  In a leadership role, it is critical to effectively manage your emotions and keep the long-term perspective in mind. This means not getting too high with wins nor too low with defeat. You will likely encounter both ends of the spectrum on a daily basis. It is important

not to let the negatives overly impact you. The role of the leader is to deal with multiple problems as they arise and maintain an even keel emotionally and a problem-solving attitude cognitively. The daily fire drills are why you have a top job. If it were easy, anyone could do it. Take the negatives in stride and solve the problem. Keep in mind that most problems get better with time, patience, and persistence.

- **Don't forget to celebrate every achievement:**
  In terms of keeping a team motivated, great leaders know the importance of celebrating achievements to keep morale high and to keep people engaged. Research by well-known business consultant Tom Peters found that the reason people stay engaged is not primarily financial. In fact, remuneration ranks below factors such as finding meaning in one's job, receiving appreciation from a manager, and receiving recognition for a job well done. As Peters said, "Celebrate what you want to see more of." When you celebrate and affirm achievements you are really celebrating and recognizing the talent you have. Never hesitate to publicly recognize and applaud the efforts behind even a small success.

- **Followers respect leaders who are both tough and kind:**
  As we have discussed, leadership is about influencing. In this sense, leaders are always balancing getting results with relationship management. It is important to keep in mind that being tough on issues but kind to people is the best approach. Very few people respect leaders who are only tough or only kind. We believe that accountability is the hallmark of an effective organization. However, accountability includes both a focus on results and a focus on the people achieving the results. Focusing exclusively on one without the other will lead to either an unproductive organization or one that seeks results at the expense of morale, which can be costly in the long term. A good leader manages both simultaneously.

- **Each medical specialty and the physicians that comprise it have their own personality and culture:**
  Earlier in this chapter, we discussed the importance of leadership versatility. Being a versatile leader means that you adjust your behavior on the basis of the role you occupy and the audience with whom you are working. The same is true when working with other physicians,

particularly in a leadership role. There are stereotypically common-alities among physicians within a specialty and differences between specialties. No doubt you have laughed at memes about this very subject while recognizing that there is some degree of truth to all the jokes. You cannot treat all physicians or specialties the same. Rather, you can only be successful treating each of them as independent en-tities. This is best illustrated in the coaching of legendary University of California at Los Angeles (UCLA) coach John Wooden. He knew that each of his players responded uniquely to different motivational tactics. He needed to be tough with some but gentle, almost fatherly, with others. He recognized that to get the maximum effort from his players, he needed to adapt his coaching to their needs.

- **Most people are consistent in their behavior**:
  If you encounter behavior that is notable in either a productive or nonproductive fashion, take note. An unexpected change in behav-ior often suggests that there has been a change in the individual's life. Changes can be the result of any number of issues, including depression, experiencing excessive pressure, and family or work problems. Regardless, it is important to have conversations as soon as you notice changes in work habits or productivity. Too often, we have seen managers ignore these problems in the hope that they will go away on their own. The results of this approach are typically disastrous. Address changes you see quickly, directly, and empathi-cally to get optimal results.

- **The best predictor of future behavior is past behavior**:
  Shakespeare noted wisely that the past is prologue to the future. Like Freud, Shakespeare knew that the best predictor of future be-havior is past behavior. This is a psychological principle on which you can rely with high levels of confidence. When you see a pattern of behaviors, assume these will continue to occur in the future. The antidote to this is an intervention in which this pattern is ad-dressed and a plan to change it is put in place by an individual mo-tivated to change. Do not expect behaviors to change on their own.

- **The team is smarter than the individual**:
  When the right group of individuals and the right leader are assem-bled to work on difficult problems, anything is possible. The talent

of the team almost always produces better results than any individual could. The challenge of the physician-leader is to gather the best talent for the problem at hand. The second challenge is to manage the group in such a way that the group's collective energy and wisdom can be harnessed and directed to solve the problems. In these circumstances, the team is always better than the skills of the individual alone.

You are about to embark on an exciting and bold transition as you move into health care leadership. As we discussed in our opening chapter, at no time in recent history has health care been in more flux. The issues are complex and divisive. No one understands health care at the grassroots level as well as the physician treating patients on a daily basis. The need to have physicians in health care leadership roles has never been greater. As you consider making this leap, we hope that you will know that we are available to help you decide if it is the right thing for you. Do not hesitate to get in touch with us. Our contact information is at the end of our biographies.

References

Goldsmith, M. 2007. *What Got You Here Won't Get You There: How Success-ful People Become Even More Successful.* New York, NY: Hyperion Press

Kaplan, R., and R. Kaiser. Summer, 2008. "Developing Versatile Leader-ship." *MIT Sloan Management Review* 44, no. 4, pp. 18–26.

About the Authors

Myron J. Beard, PhD is a business psychologist and world-class consultant, coach, and speaker. He is founder and principal of Beard Executive Consulting, a company that consults with executives on strategy development, aligning structure to strategy and executive and team development. Since he started his company in 2006, he has worked extensively with executives across industries, assisting leaders and organizations to enhance their personal and business performance.

Based in Denver, Colorado, Myron has worked with clients around the world. Clients range from small privately held companies to large multinational companies. He has worked extensively in health care, including with Anthem Blue Cross/Blue Shield (IN), Kaiser Permanente (CO), Colorado Children's Hospital, Presbyterian Healthcare (NM), Carondelet Health System (AZ), Grand River Health (CO), and Gunnison Valley Healthcare (CO). He has also worked with companies in other industries, including First Data Corporation (worldwide), Western Union Corporation (worldwide), Harnishfeger Corporation (PA), Hill's Pet Products (KS), Joy Mining Manufacturing (US, UK, Australia, South Africa), Dobson Park (UK), Longwall Corporation (Australia), KN Energy (CO), The Industrial Company (CO), Kiewit (KS), Kansas State University College of Veterinary Medicine, Nebraska Public Power District, Orica Mining Services (US, Europe, Australia, Singapore, South America), Presbyterian Health Plan (NM), Xcel Energy (MN), Public Service of NM, Montana Power Company, Cupertino Electric (CA), Ball Aerospace (CO), Best Western (AZ), Dial Corporation (AZ), TeleCheck (TX), GE Johnson Construction (CO), and Rio Rancho School District (NM).

During the course of his career, Myron has worked with thousands of executives, facilitating strategy development, helping create high-performing teams in extreme work environments, leading international merger integration efforts, and working with companies to assist them in their restructuring efforts. He has interviewed and assessed hundreds of executives for development and promotion and hiring decisions.

In 2018, he coauthored *The DNA of Leadership,* and in 2007, he coauthored *Merger Integration: a CEO's Field Guide to the Art & Process of Effective Merger Integration.* He has also authored numerous articles and book chapters.

He can be e-mailed at MyronBeard@BeardExecutiveConsulting.com

Dr. Steve Quach has been the chief executive officer at CarePoint Health since January 2016. CarePoint Health is a multispecialty physician group that is based in Colorado and Utah but provides services across the nation. Dr. Quach was previously the chief medical officer at Presbyterian/St. Luke's Medical Center (P/SL), where he gained nearly three years of tenure. Prior to his P/SL CMO appointment, he served as vice president and chief medical officer for the University of Texas Medical Branch (UTMB) Health System in Galveston, Texas, since the beginning of 2009.

Dr. Quach received his medical degree from UTMB, where he also completed both his internship and residency before serving as chief resident in his final year. He is board certified in Internal Medicine, and his primary professional interests include physician-leadership development and quality improvement in health care delivery.

Dr. Quach's experience in health care quality improvement includes leading a team in submission of an application for the Malcolm Baldrige National Quality Award to the University of Texas Center for Performance Excellence in 2006. He served as Director of Quality Management for the Department of Internal Medicine at UTMB from 2006 through 2009. His training in the field of health care quality improvement includes completion of the Advanced Training Program, conducted by Intermountain Healthcare. Dr. Quach received certification as a patient safety officer on completion of this program. From a leadership development perspective, he is proud to have founded the Physician-Leadership Academy at UTMB and was part of the leadership team that was responsible for developing the curriculum. He has extensive experience developing, mentoring, and coaching leaders both internal and external.

He can be e-mailed at: sqquach@comcast.net

Index

OTHER TITLES IN OUR HEALTHCARE MANAGEMENT COLLECTION

David Dilts, Oregon Health & Science University (OHSU)
and Lawrence Fredendall, Clemson University, *Editors*

- *Quality Management in a Lean Health Care Environment* by Daniel Collins and Melissa Mannon
- *Improving Healthcare Management at the Top: How Balanced Boardrooms Can Lead to Organizational Success* by Milan Frankl and Sharon Roberts
- *The Patient Paradigm Shifts: Profiling the New Healthcare Consumer* by Judy L. Chan
- *Leading Adaptive Teams in Healthcare Organizations* by Kurt C. O'Brien and Christopher E. Johnson
- *Management Skills for Clinicians, Volume I: Transitioning to Administration* by Linda R. LaGanga
- *Management Skills for Clinicians, Volume II: Advancing Your Skills* by Linda R. LaGanga

Announcing the Business Expert Press Digital Library

Concise e-books business students need for classroom and research

This book can also be purchased in an e-book collection by your library as

- a one-time purchase,
- that is owned forever,
- allows for simultaneous readers,
- has no restrictions on printing, and
- can be downloaded as PDFs from within the library community.

Our digital library collections are a great solution to beat the rising cost of textbooks. E-books can be loaded into their course management systems or onto students' e-book readers.

The **Business Expert Press** digital libraries are very affordable, with no obligation to buy in future years. For more information, please visit **www.businessexpertpress.com/librarians**. To set up a trial in the United States, please email **sales@businessexpertpress.com**.

CPSIA information can be obtained
at www.ICGtesting.com
Printed in the USA
FFHW011637031219
56477723-62281FF